The Art of the Footnote

THE ART OF THE FOOTNOTE[1]

The Intelligent Student's Guide to the Art and Science of Annotating Texts

Francis A. Burkle-Young

&

Saundra Rose Maley

University Press of America, Inc.

---

1. "**Foot-note**. . . . A note or comment inserted at the foot of the text. Hence **Foot-note** *v*., to furnish with a foot-note or foot-notes; to comment on in a foot-note" (*Oxford English Dictionary*).

Copyright © 1996 by
University Press of America,® Inc.
4720 Boston Way
Lanham, Maryland 20706

3 Henrietta Street
London, WC2E 8LU England

Library of Congress Cataloging-in-Publication Data

Burkle-Young, Francis A.
The art of the footnote : the intelligent student's guide to the art and
science of annotating texts / Francis A. Burkle-Young & Saundra Rose
Maley
p.   cm.
Includes bibliographical references and index.
1. Bibliographical citations. 2. Plagiarism. I. Maley, Saundra. II.
Title.
PN171.F56B87   1996   808'.027--dc20   96-16362   CIP

ISBN 0-7618-0347-5 (cloth: alk. ppr.)
ISBN 0-7618-0348-3 (pbk: alk. ppr.)

To the Memory of

ELLEN LOUISE BURKLE YOUNG
(1905-1979)

Contents

Preface

WE CAME to write this book after years of experience in the classroom, where we meet so many students who are unable, in the slightest way, to document or comment upon the materials that they found in doing research for small freshman term papers. Indeed, we find that most students, and many published writers, today cannot distinguish the use of factual matters that are taken from secondary sources from plagiarism itself. The commonly-held idea that a paraphrase of someone else's writing automatically exculpates the later writer from any imputation of plagiarism is so widespread as to be a real blight on the process of research and writing. One distinguished professor of our acquaintance, at a major Eastern university, has stopped assigning the research paper to his undergraduate students altogether, because he has found that they cannot, apparently, avoid plagiarizing, simply because they have no firm idea of precisely what plagiarism is.[1] This little book will contribute in some measure to the reduction of this pernicious habit, because it tells students exactly how to document all of the materials they encounter in doing their research. If every source for every fact or assertion is documented fully, and if additional materials are offered to readers to supplement the original body of sources, then the use of unattributed facts and statements practically disappears.

For many years past, the defense of the footnote seemed almost hopeless. Protestations that students and writers needed to document their sources fully, and that additional or secondary information and commentary needed to be included in formal papers as a guide to fuller understanding, was met with derision, even in academic circles. In more recent years, however, with

---

1. So widespread has this practice become that major publishers are issuing volumes whose authors have cribbed most of their material from published works without attribution—offering to their readers as their own work the labors of others. One particular example of this is Craig M. Carver, *A History of English in Its Own Words* (New York: HarperCollins, 1991), in which he presents the information contained in entries in the *Oxford English Dictionary*, with the abbreviations extended and the prose ramified, as his own scholarship.

the increasing concern for standards of academic ethics and honesty, the fully-documented paper once again seems very desirable, indeed. And, when this small revolution against the decay of scholarly standards is coupled with the ease with which wordprocessors handle the creation of footnotes, the way is ready for students and general writers alike to return to the well-documented and well-commented expository paper. Perhaps the clearest expression of the tendency towards shoddy scholarship that is promoted by the lack of documentation came from Gertrude Himmelfarb in her sharply crafted essay, "Where Have All the Footnotes Gone?"[2] Today, we hear many of our colleagues speak more and more about the need to make students aware of the established and traditional pathways for expressing scholarly honesty and indebtedness, yet we also hear of the complete absence of any guide for students which will relieve college and university instructors of the need to take many hours of class time to explain to their students just how to accomplish the task.

It has been said that one of the best methods for learning how to follow a blazed trail is to blaze one yourself. By offering students and writers a means to present complete documentation, as well as a guide to all of the many other functions of the footnote, including, most importantly, the presentation of contrasting or opposing points of view, we hope to enhance, in some small degree, the present trend towards a restoration of traditional academic ethics and responsibility, not only in academic writing but also in general articles and books. We know of no better means for displaying intellectual honesty than by a full and unabashed presentation of one's processes of research. As Robinson Crusoe followed the footprints of Friday to his discovery, each reader should have the opportunity, if she wishes, to follow the whole process of research which underlies a term paper, journal article, thesis, or dissertation, with ease and clarity.

2. Gertrude Himmelfarb, "Where Have All the Footnotes Gone?" *New York Times* (16 June 1991) §7 Book Review, p. 1, col. 1; revised and expanded in *On Looking Into the Abyss: Untimely Thoughts on Culture and Society* (New York: Alfred A. Knopf, 1994) 122–130.

As we explain in detail later, footnotes offer the writer a sure method for keeping each paper, article, or book, no matter how complex or ramified, in the form of a seamless essay, in the best traditions of the eighteenth and nineteenth centuries. The writer's text flows smoothly from its introductory matter, through the exposition, to its conclusion, without any interruption of the flow of the discourse. All secondary material—explanatory notes, comments, asides, and digressions, as well as the source material—is placed in footnotes, with only the smallest superscripted number to displace the eye and the mind of the reader from the task of reading.

To provide students and writers with a respectable guide to using footnotes, we could not do better than to select examples of the various types of notes as models for general imitation. We have chosen our samples from a wide range of authorship, from the freshman term paper, through the doctoral dissertation, to the masterworks of great writers and scholars. We also selected examples from the broadest possible spectrum of writing—not just works in English language and literature, but also works of history, mathematics, physics, art, biology, and texts on general research, among others.

A brief note on the formatting of the texts which follow is necessary here. We have kept, in almost every instance, the style of citation that the author of each of our examples chose to use. Consequently, there is some variation in the interior citations and the bibliographical abbreviations. In some cases, we have extended the abbreviations and citations in the notes, because the notes themselves used shortened forms, when they were not the first notes in a work to cite a source. In addition, we have, in a few cases, used examples which were endnotes when they were first published; and we have omitted some notes in our examples which are associated with the texts we chose, in order to highlight the examples more clearly.

Acknowledgments

First, we wish to acknowledge our debt to several of our own mentors who, as masters of the profession of scholar-teacher, imbued us with an understanding of the importance of rigorous scholarship together with a devotion to intellectual honesty and openness. These present and former professors at the University of Maryland at College Park are vividly in our memory: the late Hermann Everard Schuessler, George Allan Cate, Clifford M. Foust, Harold Herman, W. Milne Holton, Leonard Lutwack, George P. Majeska, Michael J. Pelczar, and William S. Peterson. And we also wish to acknowledge that the impetus for this book stems directly from the principles of scholarship and the elevated standards of ethics and openness of the late Mrs. Ellen Louise Burkle-Young, once the editor and publisher of the *Jamestown Courier* and later a valuable member of the staff of the Division of Mechanical and Civil Engineering of the Smithsonian Institution and of the American Law Division of the Legislative Reference Service of the Library of Congress. The most readily accessible examples of her work are perhaps to be found in her many articles for the fourteenth revised edition of the *Encyclopædia Britannica*.

Although we understand that the examples we have used do fall under the ægis of the doctrine of fair use, we do wish to express our acknowledgment to the authors and publishers of these works. They represent fine standards of traditional, rigorous scholarship which provide the modern student with excellent models.

We also wish to thank our students of the past, who have entered enthusiastically into the methods and philsophy of research we try to teach. Some examples from their freshman and sophomore term papers enhance this book. Among these students are Mr. Jan Robert Danielsen (University of Maryland), Ms. Johanna C. Cullen (George Mason University), Mr. John Montgomery Bishop (University of Maryland), Mr. Neal Paulsen (The George Washington University), and Mr. Mariusz R. Grabek (The George Washington University).

Mr. Grabek is especially to be thanked, for he gave freely of many hours of his time to help us to retrieve texts from several libraries, to proofread large portions of the manuscript, and to offer valuable suggestions from an undergraduate perspective.

Our thanks also to Dr. Thomas Mann of the General Reference

and Bibliography Division of the Library of Congress in Washington and author of *A Guide to Library Research Methods*. Dr. Mann encouraged us greatly in our work and was most helpful to us in our initial search for a publisher.

Finally, we wish to acknowledge our deepest debt to Professor William S. Peterson of the University of Maryland. In addition to his broad and unwavering encouragement for this project, he designed and typeset the book. Without his assistance, we could not have offered our readers so attractive and so readable a volume, including, as it does, so many typographical difficulties caused by so great a variety of form, from elaborate mathematical notation to texts and notes in non-Latin characters. We also are very conscious of the fact that through his participation in our project, our little book can take a small place in the genealogy of the printed word in descent from William Morris and from Morris's great mentor, the foremost exemplar of the understanding of the sense of beauty, John Ruskin.

Some Preliminaries

THE PURPOSE of this little book is to reacquaint students and writers with the footnote as the most effective method for presenting all of the information that is necessary to make every manuscript lucid for every reader. We hope to show why footnotes are valuable, even essential, as a part of writing in the context of the scientific and historical methods of research; how easy it is to become thoroughly familiar with the various types of notes and when to employ them; and how to create footnotes which are both clear and helpful to the reader.

Most people today are familiar with the principal elements of the scientific method: that the order and course of each experiment must be documented with sufficient completeness to allow the experiment to be repeated, under the same conditions, with the same results. The principal tenets of the traditional historical method are less well known today, but, essentially, they are the same: the presentation must include all of the information that is necessary for the reader to follow precisely in the footsteps of the writer, to provide a full understanding of how the writer reached her conclusion. In this case, of course, it is not necessary for the reader to reach the same conclusion, from the same material, that the original writer did, but the reader must be able to understand clearly how the original writer reached the conclusion she did.

Every non-fictional work is, or ought to be, an immediate personal communication from the writer to each of her readers. When this writing is most effective, it is a clear, seamless expository essay, with no digressions to distract the attention of the reader from the essential points of the discourse. It does not matter, inherently, whether the work is a ten-page undergraduate term paper or a major exposition of a weighty topic in a monograph of six hundred pages or more, the principle remains the same. Because this is the case, all those complementary elements, the interruptions or parenthetical expressions of thought, should be removed from the main text and placed in some convenient location to which the reader can refer, if she wishes to do so; or ignored altogether, if the reader wishes only to come to a swift understanding of the author's main points. Only in this way can the seamless quality of the expression be preserved.

Footnotes are, in a sense, the footprints of the author in the sands of research, analysis, and writing. They make it possible for each reader to follow the author's physical steps in research as well as the progress of her analysis. Each new element of complementary information, which the author thought was necessary to her own understanding of her topic, can be found by the reader, as well.

Footnotes are meant to be ignored by the reader who has only a casual interest in the topic or a limited time for its consideration. That is precisely why they are indicated by small superscripted numbers in the text. They need not even break the flow of the eye across the page. Often, in former times, it was common for a serious reader to give a work a first perusal in which she ignored the footnotes altogether. Later, she would revisit the text for a second reading, with a full consideration of those notes she found to be useful for her own understanding. Of course, as you would, yourself, she was likely to do this only if she found the material valuable or exciting, or both. With this approach, the uninterrupted flow of the main text becomes a type of epitome or synopsis of the author's research and analysis and the footnotes complete the whole exposition of the writer's work and thought. If the reader wishes to elaborate her understanding of the topic and the author's consideration of it, she has the footnotes at her disposal to ease her labors.

In reading the footnotes, each reader makes her own judgment about which of them contains information that is useful to her. The footnotes, in effect, are the means by which the author tailors her text to the more precise needs and desires of each of her potential readers. They can be ignored altogether, by the casual reader, or all of them can receive a full consideration, from the reader who aspires to a similar, or even more extensive, scholarship—from the reader on the bus to the dedicated graduate student.

In a world of increasingly large volumes of information, no

one reader, however well educated, can be expected to know the background of any particular paper or essay; so that the author may think that she has a scholarly need to elucidate every point she can in the text. At the same time, every author has the obligation to present her work in a readily-accessible way. It is the inherent conflict between these desires that has led to the war between the writers for a select, informed audience, on the one hand, and those writers who claim that a work is successful only if every reader understands the material easily and fully, on the other. *The Art of the Footnote* attempts to show how these positions, which appear to conflict with one another, can be reconciled, so that the author can be successful in documenting her work to the satisfaction of even her most meticulous reader, and every reader can extract all of the information she desires from the text.

Today, it is common to omit those details of research and investigation which allow a reader to retrace, with ease and exactitude, the precise steps that an author has taken in her research. Yet, as we will show, this is the fundamental purpose of scholarly notation.

*

Since footnotes originally were a convention of printing, they were always difficult to arrange and format in a typescript. Consequently, from the later nineteenth century to within the past few years, the authors of style manuals increasingly have recommended easier and easier methods for including information in papers, without the use of the full scholarly note. Thus, we have seen the rise of endnotes and parenthetical citations. Footnotes have decided advantages over them, however. If a reader wishes to use footnotes, they are present just below the material to which they refer, or which they amplify or define. Endnotes, by contrast, are removed physically from the material to which they relate, which forces the reader to flip back and forth from the text to the notes. This, by its very nature, interrupts the flow of the discourse and, in most cases, annoys the reader with another task that is unrelated to reading or to digesting the text and the material that is associated directly with it. Parenthetical notes, too, break up the flow of the text and can hardly be ignored by the eye.

The widespread use of the word processor as the principal means for producing manuscripts, however, has rendered all of these suspect shortcuts obsolete. For example, the use of parenthetical notes to provide bibliographical citations serves well, when they are the only notes an author wishes to include—and, in works which are documented fully, these often amount to only about thirty percent of the material that usually is included in notes—but they provide no means at all for presenting any other sort of information, other than the bibliographical. With modern word processing software, the presentation of all the "notable" material can be done with a keystroke, and removes from any manuscript the annoying and distracting parenthetical notes, which interrupt the flow of the discourse.

We should say a word or two here about the materials of research and experiment which do not go in footnotes. You should place in an appendix, or appendices, an extensive table or a series of tables, transcripts of documents, secondary or tertiary texts which only are tangential to your thesis, and any other matter which will take more than a single-spaced page for its presentation or explanation.

We also need to indicate the place where the author places the sign for a footnote. The number, or symbol, for the note is inserted either immediately after the mark of punctuation which follows the word or phrase the author is noting—typically this is at the end of the sentence which contains the item to be noted—or immediately after the word or term which the writer wishes to note. The latter placement always is the case when the author provides a definition for an unusual word or when she provides a translation of a word to or from a foreign language.

Footnotes, properly conceived and properly placed, provide the one means by which every writer can document thoroughly the methods and directions of her research, so that each reader can follow the author's work and thought precisely. In this way, footnotes serve as a guarantee of intellectual honesty; because they promote a spirit of openness and fairness in the scholarly community for the spread and consideration of research and ideas; and they provide a full and thorough documentation for later investigations, experiments, and study.

Finally, footnotes actually are notes to the reader. They are the author's way of addressing her audience directly, quite like an actor who makes an aside in a play—a monologue, not a soliloquy. Footnotes include all of those sorts of asides and comments which would take place normally in a discursive conversation, but which generally should not appear in the main body of a formal essay. One surviving sign of the fact that the footnote really is a personal note to the reader is that bibliographical citations in notes are full sentences, and have a very different appearance from their form in bibliographies or lists of works cited. The bibliographical footnote has one period only, at the end of the "sentence" that is the complete citation.

A Little Bit of History

THE PRESENCE of notes in a completed text is nearly as old as writing itself. We have, for example, Egyptian papyri which have either marginal or interlinear notes, or both. Of course, in the age of manuscripts, such notes generally were used to correct or emend errors in the text, rather than to amplify information. In addition, the owners of manuscripts often would add marginalia to indicate the topic under discussion in the main text. Both of these habits found their first printed expression in the use of side notes. Joseph Moxon, in his *Mechanick Exercises on the whole Art of Printing*, the major work in English on printing and layout in the seventeenth century,[1] describes in detail how the printer is to set up marginal notes so that they will appear properly on the printed page. His directions are our oldest guides to the form for placing notes in a published book. Today, such brief topical guides and commentary are grouped together under the title "marginalia," because, in the old manuscript tradition, they almost always appeared in the wide margins of a manuscript's leaves. We can see them, especially, in textbooks on tightly organized subjects, where they serve to guide the student through densely written prose, all of which is regarded by the author as important.[2]

Lest the researcher fall into the error of believing that marginalia are of only secondary importance to the topic under dis-

1. Joseph Moxon, *Mechanick Exercises on the whole Art of Printing (1683–4)*, edited by Herbert Davis and Harry Carter, 2nd ed. (London: Oxford University Press, 1962). Moxon was born in Yorkshire in 1627, and became hydrographer to Charles II (1660–1685). In addition to his masterwork on printing, he published many other treatises on mathematics and navigation and made both globes and maps. He died about 1700. For additional details on the life and career of Joseph Moxon, see Herbert Davis, "The Art of Printing: Joseph Moxon and His Successors." *Printing and Graphic Arts*, 5 (1957), 17–33; and Edward Rowe Mores, *A Dissertation upon English Typographical Founders and Foundries*, ed. Harry Carter and Christopher Ricks (London: Oxford University Press, 1961).

2. One worthwhile example of this use of marginalia, or side notes, is to be found in Ronald J. Gillespie, *et al.*, *Atoms, Molecules, and Reactions: An Introduction to Chemistry* (Englewood Cliffs, New Jersey: Prentice-Hall Inter-

cussion, it is worthwhile to recall the famous statement of Fermat's Last Theorem.[3] Diophantus, in Book II, problem 8, of
his *Arithmetic* asks "given a number which is a square, write it
as the sum of two other squares." In the margin adjacent to this
statement, Fermat noted in his copy, in Latin, "On the other
hand, it is impossible for a cube to be written as a sum of two
cubes or a fourth power to be written as a sum of two fourth
powers or, in general, for any number of a power which is
greater than the second to be written as a sum of two like powers. I have a truly marvelous demonstration of this proposition
which this margin is too narrow to contain."[4] As far as we can
tell from his surviving papers, Fermat never returned to this
problem to write down his "marvelous demonstration"; and
mathematicians have been searching for his proof from his
time to our own. Recently, with all the powers of modern

---

national, Inc., 1994). In their preface (p. xviii), Gillespie and his colleagues
explain their use of two forms of marginalia, one in blue type and one in
black.

A famous example of the use of both marginalia, for topical guides, and
footnotes, for emending or amplifying information, is John Bagnell Bury's
edition of Edward Gibbon's *The History of the Decline and Fall of the Roman
Empire*, in seven brilliantly annotated volumes (London: Methuen & Co.,
Ltd., 1911).

3. Pierre de Fermat (1601–1665) a friend from youth of the even more famous Blaise Pascal, discovered a number of mathematical properties which
laid part of the groundwork for all modern study of that subject. He devised
a simpler method of quadrating parabolas than that offered by Archimedes
in the third century before Christ. He also discovered a fresh method for de-
termining the greatest and smallest ordinates of curved lines, which is anal-
ogous to, and anticipates, the methods for doing this in differential calculus.
Except for a minor appendix to another author's work, published in 1660,
Fermat steadfastly refused to publish his own work in his lifetime. After his
death, his son, Samuel, found his father's copy of a French translation of
Diophantus's Arithmetic, which was covered with Pierre's marginalia.
Samuel then published a new edition of this translation, with his father's
notes added as an appendix (*Diophanti Alexandrini arithmeticorum libri sex,
et de numeris multangulis liber unus. Cum commentariis C[laude] G[aspard] Ba-
cheti V. C. et observationibus D. P. de Fermat Senatoris Tolosani* [Tolosae: Ex-
cudebat Bernardus Bosc, e regione Collegij Societatis Iesu., 1670]).

4. Translated and discussed in Harold M. Edwards, Fermat's Last Theorem: A Genetic Introduction to Algebraic Number Theory (New York:

mathematics and the computer, the proof was discovered,[5] but the marginalium remains one of the most tantalizing in history.

Another form of early marginalia, not quite so old as emendations and topical references, are glosses. While these often took the form of brief definitions of words which were thought to be unfamiliar and, as such, became the ancestors of modern glossaries, more often they took the form of cross-references to other parts of the same text, or collections of texts, or were exegeses in the form of brief commentaries on the meaning and significance of words, phrases, or passages. We are most familiar with glosses today in their appearance in religious texts, notably the Bible and the Quran.

The beginnings of modern scholarship in the Italian Renaissance added to this collection of secondary information some notices by the author of his sources and the specific references he made to them. Footnotes, or bottom-notes as they were first called, represent a compromise between the desire of the author to indicate his sources and annotate his material with the printer's desire to present an orderly and well-formatted page.[6] Soon, it became conventional to print the footnotes in a type that was one or two sizes smaller than that used for the main body of the text. This convention remains with us today.

Because the footnotes applied specifically to the material on the same page, it was unlikely that any author would produce

---

Springer-Verlag, 1977), 2. In modern notation, Fermat asserts that, for any integer n > 2, the equation xn+yn=zn is impossible.

5. For the full exposition of the proof, see Andrew Wiles in *Annals of Mathematics* (Princeton), May, 1995, where his elucidation takes the entire issue of two hundred pages. For a more popular and accessible account, see Gina Kolata, "How a Gap in the Fermat Proof was Bridged," *New York Times* (31 January 1995), §C Science Desk, p. 1, col. 4.

6. The oldest use of the word footnote in English is in William Savage, *A Dictionary of the Art of Printing* (London: Longman, Brown, Green, and Longmans, 1841), 88, s.v. Bottom Notes: "The notes at the bottom or foot of a page. The are usually composed in a type two sizes smaller than that used for the body of the work: thus, if the work be printed with a Pica type, the notes will be composed in Long Primer; if with English, the notes will be Small Pica. They are also termed *Foot Notes*."

more than six of them for any one page of text. Consequently, printers soon developed a nearly-universal convention of signs to indicate the order of the notes. In order, from the first note to the sixth, these signs were the asterisk (*), the obelisk or dagger (†), the double dagger (‡), the section sign (§), the parallel (||) and the paraph (¶). While this was a regular and orderly method for presenting the notes on a page, and was typographically satisfying, as well, it was difficult to make cross-references to these notes at other points in the text, because there was no absolute identifier for each note. Printers experimented with several other systems of annotational signs, including lower case letters in italics, but eventually they settled on a sequential numbering of the notes, in superscript characters, which ran for the whole length of an article, a chapter, or an entire book.[7] One older form of footnoting which survives in some modern examples is the method called "keyword noting." When this method is used, a word or a short phrase from the main body of the text is quoted in italics as the indicator of the footnote.[8]

The presence of footnotes on the page of a printed book depended for its layout and appearance on the skills of the typesetter. As long as he, and he alone, had to do the work, footnotes presented few problems for authors. The invention of the practical typewriter in the late 1860's, however, brought a whole new realm of difficulty to the use and presentation of footnotes.[9] The new invention made everyman his own printer, and brought to every typist the same problems that typesetters had

7. For an early discussion of the signs used for footnotes and the various systems for using them, see Savage, *op. cit.*, 700–701.

8. Herbert Davis and Harry Carter, in their edition of *Moxon's Mechanick Exercises* (see note 1 above), use *keyword footnoting* to annotate the original author's very technical text.

9. Christopher Latham Sholes (1819–1890) is often called, with considerable justice, the "father of the typewriter." In 1867, he, together with two of his colleagues, Samuel W. Soulé and Carlos Glidden, invented and patented a device which was, in effect, a small portable printing press. Within a few years, he and others made mechanical improvements to the device which caused it to supersede the handwritten manuscript for nearly all business and academic purposes, leaving the traditional form only for personal correspondence.

learned to overcome through years of training and experience. For example, authors for many years had indicated in their manuscripts those parts of their texts which they wished to have printed in italics by underlining them. This custom was transferred easily to typewriting, and underlining quickly became the normal method for indicating those parts of a text which would be in italics if printed, such as the titles of books and the names of ships. Other typographical conventions, however, did not take to adaptation quite so well. The superscript numbers which indicated a footnote required the typist to move the machine's platen back a half-step, to achieve the superscript. In addition, the typist had to measure the space at the bottom of each typed page carefully, to ensure that there would be enough room to accommodate the text of the footnote. Each page became, in effect, a bedeviling exercise in typography done by the rankest amateur. If a note had to be changed in a printed text, the typesetter merely removed the old number and inserted the new, both in the text and at the front of the note. When the typist had to perform the same act, she had to erase both the numbers she had typed, very carefully, and then type the new numbers over the site of the old ones. The fragility of the paper inherently limited her ability to make such changes to, at most, two for the same note. After this, if she were faced with the same problem, she had to retype the whole page.

Thus, while the concept of "everyman his own printer" seemed very attractive, indeed, in reality it led to a degree of frustration which was beyond anything that might be encountered in a handwritten manuscript, in which numbers could be crossed out at will and the notes themselves generally were on separate pages when they were delivered to the printer.

Very quickly, authors began to search for new conventions that were applicable specifically to typewriting, and which would obviate the need to be a fully-trained typographer in order to produce a well-formed page. Endnotes, either at the end of a chapter or at the back of the whole book, made it possible for typists to avoid the careful measurement of pages to accommodate space for the footnotes, although the problems of renumbering, whenever the author added or deleted a note, still remained. Endnotes also created a new distraction for the reader. To consult them, the reader had to thumb back and forth constantly, from the page of text to the page with the relevant notes. But, at least, the endnote allowed the author to retain all of the information which had appeared traditionally in the footnote.[10]

The next development in this process, the parenthetical citation, sacrificed information to the cause of speed and ease of typing. Unfortunately, because such citations can indicate only bibliographical sources or present very short commentaries, they rob the writer of her ability to present all of the annotations which are necessary to document the manuscript fully, to achieve the maximum degree of clarity, and to preserve complete intellectual honesty. In addition to this, the presence of references in parentheses breaks up the flow of the author's essay and creates a series of choppy phrases, which often are not easy on either the eye or the concentration of the reader. Indeed, the presence of these citations presents a much more cluttered page to the reader's eye than ever was the case with the superscripted numbers for footnotes.

By about 1980, the use of notes had been reduced in scope to include only the briefest of bibliographical citations and very little else. All the other information that might enhance the presentation of the author's ideas and that documented her research and analysis had been sacrificed to make it possible for the typist to prepare a manuscript without any particular typographical knowledge. The reader's ability to understand fully the whole journey that the author had taken was diminished greatly. And secondary and tertiary material which once would have been relegated properly to a note now had to be incorpo-

10. Of course, like every other invention, endnotes have a pioneer. Jean Jacques Rousseau, in his Second Discourse, appended all of his curious and ramified notes to the end of his text, where they form the last seventy-seven pages of his book. See Jean Jacques Rousseau, *Discours sur l'origine et les fondemens de l'inégalité parmi les hommes* (Amsterdam: Chez Marc Michel Rey, 1755). For a comment on Rousseau's notes, and on notation in general, see Gertrude Himmelfarb, "Where Have All the Footnotes Gone?," *New York Times* (16 June 1991), §7 Book Review, p. 1, col. 1.

rated into the main body of the text, if the author wished to include it at all—which further impeded the seamless flow of good expository writing.

One of the first applications of digital technology to win acceptance, with enthusiasm, in the workplace was the word processor. Early machines that were dedicated to that purpose soon gave way to word processing software for the microcomputer. Within two years after the introduction of efficient microcomputers, software for word processing was one of the two or three most frequently used applications for them. Programs such as *WordStar* and *MultiMate* quickly added a feature to their software which inserted footnotes automatically. By the late 1980s, all word processing programs of any importance had included the ability to do this; and to reformat each page to place the notes properly. The software, in effect, now embodied the whole range of expertise in footnoting that once was possessed only by the skilled typesetter.

With the microcomputer, it is now possible to restore the full range of annotations to every term paper, article, and book—almost effortlessly. The author now, once again, can reveal her depth of scholarship, her detailed exposition of research and analysis, her presentation of secondary or contrasting information, or points of view, to reëstablish the evidence of intellectual integrity which caused the footnote to be developed in the first place. It is now easier to use footnotes than it has ever been in the history of writing manuscripts. They can be incorporated into any text with, at most, a few keystrokes.[11]

On the pages which follow, we describe some specific cases in which footnoting is appropriate and we illustrate those with examples that we have drawn from a variety of writings, from undergraduate term papers to large monographs which embody distinguished scholarship.

---

11. In an appendix, we include instructions for creating footnoting macros for many of the major word processing programs.

A Very Biassed Note on Notes

NOW THAT YOU have read how the footnote came into existence, and then how the various other forms of annotations evolved from it, we think that you are owed a little explanation of why the modern writer should prefer to use footnotes rather than other notational forms.

The two principal points in favor of the footnote are its visual immediacy and its freedom from obscurity. The first point is, in general, self-evident. The footnote lies primarily on the same page as the material you are annotating, ready and available to your reader without the need to turn pages to find the information elsewhere. Even the longest footnote seldom will run more than some lines into the note area on the following page. By contrast, the endnote, whether you place it at the end of a chapter or section, or place it at the end of the full text, holds the information at some distance from the convenient eye of your reader. Indeed, the very reader whose sympathy you wish to capture, or whose intellect you wish to engage with your own, may well be distracted by her search for the place where you put your notes, and then by her further search among your collection for the precise note that she wishes to consult.

But the endnote does afford you the opportunity to present your secondary and complementary information thoroughly and completely, however annoying it may be for your reader to find it. The parenthetical citation places both you and your reader in a mutually confusing position. First, such notes usually are restricted to noting bibliographical sources, which gives little scope to all of the many other sorts of information which the footnote can hold. Consequently, all of those other asides, biographical or geographical details, descriptions, opinions, and comments, must be placed in the main body of your text, if they are to appear at all. Quite often, this will force you to abandon the essential foundation of all good expository writing—a seamless, clear, and coherent essay, in which each point of discussion flows from the one before it, without distraction or fluctuation. All those wonderful details and interesting sidelights which you discovered in your research and found so fascinating, those very minor points of excitement which made your own work so interesting, must be omitted from your final text, because, if you do include them, your paper may well appear to be very choppy and, in the worst cases, incoherent.

It seems to us that if you wish to keep the interest and enthusiasm of your reader throughout the whole reading of your text, distracting her with digressions from the mainstream of your thesis is hardly a good way to do it. And yet this is what you must do, if you wish to include explanations and information that is secondary, yet important, to an understanding of your text, and if you are encumbered by a commitment to the parenthetical form of annotation. But, with the footnote at hand, your reader can move smoothly through your writing, with unchecked concentration; ignoring, if she wishes, those tiny numbers that float into view from time to time; yet she also can drop her eyes to the additional information and commentary you have provided, if she chances upon a curious point, or one that seems, at first glance, challengeable, or even bizarre.

Beyond this consideration, however, lies the weakness of the parenthetical citation as a guide to further discovery by your reader. Consider the following passage:

> Once the reasoning of modern forensic pathology began to be applied to the circumstances of Napoleon's last months and days on St. Helena, including discussions of the possibilities of arsenic poisoning (Forshufvud and Weider, 1978, 1995; Weider, 1982), the deterioration caused by his thrombosed hemorrhoids (Welling, *et al.*, 1988), and the nature of his recurrent apnea (Chouard, *et al.*, 1988), historians were forced to reconsider seriously the nature of his final illness and the actual cause of his death.

We think that many readers will find this passage unsatisfying. First, the text is broken in several places by interjections, the parenthetical references, that break the flow of reading and threaten concentration. Second, the reader who does wish to know more about these subjects must go to the bibliography at the end of the work and thumb through it to get the citations to which the references apply. After this, if she obtains the books and articles, she must peruse their indices to try to determine just where the author got the material she so quickly noted— and if one or more of the longer works has no index, the problem becomes significantly more difficult. In this light, it is somewhat ironic that the leading manual of style which advocates the use of parenthetical notes should state that, unless they "strengthen the discussion," footnotes should not be used "because they are distracting to readers and expensive to include in printed material."[1] The latter comment is particularly specious, because almost all printing and publishing today is set directly from digitized files, and the cost of the content of one page is precisely the same as the cost of the content of any other, unless graphical images are included. It also seems to our eye that having sentences broken repeatedly with parenthetical citations is much more distracting than the presence of a small, superscripted number at the end of the sentence. Finally, any material which strengthens your discussion should be placed, at all times, in the main body of your text.

Now let us look at the same passage again, with the addition of a bibliographical footnote with some added detail:

> Once the reasoning of modern forensic pathology began to be applied to the circumstances of Napoleon's last months and days on St. Helena, including discussions of the possibilities of arsenic poisoning, the deterioration caused by his thrombosed hemorrhoids, and the nature of his recurrent apnea, historians were forced to reconsider seriously the nature of his final illness and the actual cause of his death.[2]

1. Publication Manual of the American Psychological Association, 4th ed. (Washington, D.C.: American Psychological Association, 1994) 163.
2. For a lengthy discussion of the possibility that Napoleon was poisoned deliberately by arsenic, see Sten Forshufvud and Ben Weider, *Assassination at St. Helena: The Poisoning of Napoleon Bonaparte* (Vancouver: Mitchell Press, 1978) and their sequel, *Assassination at St. Helena Revisited* (New York: John Wiley & Sons, 1995). See also, for a recent medical opinion, the letter of M. Keynes, "Did Napoleon Die from Arsenical Poisoning," *Lancet*, vol. 344, no. 8917 (22 July 1994): 276. On his thrombosed hemorrhoidal prolapse, see D. R. Welling, B. G. Wolff, and R. R. Dozois, "Piles of Defeat: Napoleon at Waterloo," *Diseases of the Colon and Rectum*, vol. 31, no. 4 (April, 1988): 303–305. And for a consideration of the possibility that he suffered from sleep apnea,

What earlier had seemed a very long sentence, broken into pieces by citations, now seems shorter, more coherent, and clearly logical in its structure. And only the tiny, superscripted numeral at the end invites the reader to glance below to learn about the sources for the statements. Of course, if the text is only of passing interest to the reader, the tiny numeral will go unregarded, as the reader pushes on to the conclusion of the paper. If the reader does, however, wish to learn more, her downward glance conveys very quickly still more information than just the bare citations. She will learn, at once and with no scrabbling to the bibliography, that the text which discusses Napoleon's possible apnea was written in French and, if she does not read that language, she can dismiss it from further consideration immediately. She also will learn that the text that was published in 1995 by Horshufvud and Weider was a direct sequel to their earlier work of 1978. And she will find a mention of a short modern medical comment on their thesis that was published in the leading British medical journal, something which was just too minor to be crowded into the parenthetical citations, yet one which considers the matter from a slightly different view. Finally, especially if she is reading the work under some pressure, for a course, an examination, or a project, she might find a smile in the somewhat wry humor of D. R. Welling and his colleagues in entitling their paper, "Piles of Defeat."

This example illustrates only a few of the many reasons for preferring a footnote, or even an endnote, to the parenthetical citation.

Once again, we ask that you always remember that the *no* in *note* is the same *no* in *know*. Both words, and such words as *acknowledge*, which also are pertinent to this book, originate in an ancient Indo-European verbal stem, *gno**, which meant *know*. That ancient root also provided Gothic with *knaian*, and its descendant, Old High German, with *cnaan* (hence modern German *kennen*); provided Old Slavic with the stem *zna* (hence

---

see C. Chouard, B. Meyer, and F. Chabolle, "Napoleon souffrait-il du syndrom d'apnée du sommeil?," *Annales d'Otolaryngologie et de Chirurgie Cervicofaciale*, vol. 105, no. 4 (1988): 299ff.

modern Russian *znat*); provided Anglo-Saxon with *cnawan* (hence our own modern English word *know*); provided Greek with the stem γνω (γνωμον and γνωσιο, among other words)[3] which has, in turn, given many modern languages words derived from it, including, in English, *Gnostic, agnostic,* and *ignorant.*[4] More particularly, for our purpose, is the knowledge that the Latin word that is involved in all of this evolution is the transitive verb *nosco, noscere, noui, notum.*[5] One of several nouns that the Romans derived from this verb was *nota, notae,* which meant a mark to indicate something that was *known,* or *to be known.*[6] This word is the ancestor of our modern English word *note,* and, hence, its descendant, the word *footnote.* We made this little journey into etymology to emphasize, once again, that the purpose of all your notes is to allow your readers to *know* what you *know,* in the fullest possible way with the least amount of difficulty. This is at the heart of the openness and honesty which should characterize the intellectual and academic life—and, ideally, life itself.

3. For a much longer discussion of the stem and the words connected to it, see Henry George Liddell and Robert Scott, *A Greek-English Lexicon,* 9th ed., rev. and aug. by Henry Stuart Jones (Oxford: Clarendon Press, 1940) 354‒355.

4. For a detailed consideration of the relationship of the ancient stem to modern words in all Indo-European languages that connote *knowledge,* see the *Oxford English Dictionary,* 2d ed., 20 vols. (Oxford: Clarendon Press, 1989) s. v. *know.*

5. P. G. W. Glare, ed., *Oxford Latin Dictionary,* combined ed. (Oxford: Clarendon Press, 1990) 1190‒1191.

6. *ibid.,* 1191‒1192, and precisely cognate with the Greek γνωμον, in the sense of *mark* or *token,* from the original connotation, *a means of knowing.* See *Liddel and Scott,* 354.

Bibliographical Footnotes

BIBLIOGRAPHICAL NOTES include, of course, references to more than just secondary matter that has been printed in books. These notes are your opportunity to point your reader to articles in journals and newspapers, interviews, speeches, lectures, film, telephone conversations; letters, diaries, and manuscripts; sources in literature, including the Bible; and, increasingly, online data and information.

All of these citations must contain the complete collection of information which allows your reader to go directly to your source with the least trouble. Do not force your reader to guess at the full title of a work, or which edition you have used; do not force her to labor to determine the date of a radio or television interview, or which version of a film you have seen.

To reduce the possibility that your reader may become confused about the information you have included, all of your bibliographical citations should be uniform in the way you present them. This you can do by adhering strictly to one style of presentation, *i.e.* to the format shown in one particular style manual.

Use the style manual which is prescribed by your publisher, university, college, department, or professor. If no one prescribes or recommends a manual to you, then perhaps your best choice is the standard manual by Kate L. Turabian, *A Manual for Writers of Term Papers, Theses, and Dissertations.*[1] Portions of the current edition of *Turabian,* as the work generally is known, are based upon the thirteenth edition of an even more impressive and famous standard, *The Chicago Manual of Style.*[2] For writers who wish to use the latest edition of the most accepted manual, a fourteenth edition of the *Chicago Manual* was published in 1993.[3] This edition is significant, because it offers, for

1. Kate L. Turabian, *A Manual for Writers of Term Papers, Theses, and Dissertations,* 5th ed., revised and expanded by Bonnie Birtwhistle Honigsblum (Chicago: The University of Chicago Press, 1987).
2. *The Chicago Manual of Style,* 13th ed., revised and expanded (Chicago: The University of Chicago Press, 1982).
3. *The Chicago Manual of Style,* 14th ed. (Chicago: The University of Chicago Press, 1993).

the first time, the formats for citing various forms of information that are stored on electronic media.[4]

Whatever manual you choose, do adhere strictly to its requirements for all of your citations.

In general, the horizontal hierarchy of your bibliographical information should progress from the most significant elements to the least significant, in terms of your reader's physical search for the work you have cited. Thus, the author's name and the title of the work come first; followed by information on the edition, the editor, or the reviser, if any; then the publication information, which includes the place of publication, the publisher, and the date of publication. Last, you indicate the volume number, if appropriate, and the page number or numbers. These last elements are valuable only after your reader has secured the item to which you refer. The logic is precise. And, of course, a single bibliographic citation is a single, complete sentence. It opens with a capitalized word—generally the first name of the author—and closes with a period, just as every other complete sentence does. This form is quite different from the way in which you list works in a bibliography, or a list of works cited, at the end of your paper, thesis, or dissertation.

In preparing bibliographical citations, there are a number of conventional abbreviations which are used regularly. You should become familiar with them, and employ them properly. See appendix B for a list of those which writers use most frequently. Take note that, in all those abbreviations which are derived from Latin or Italian, the plural form of the abbreviation doubles the primary letter used for it. Thus, *p* for *page* and *pp* for *pages*, *v* for *verse* and *vv* for *verses*, *MS* for *manuscript* and *MSS* for *manuscripts*.

---

4. Until a new edition of a major manual of style addresses the issue of citing information that is stored and retrieved electronically, the *de facto* standard is Xia Li and Nancy B. Crane, *Electronic Style: A Guide to Citing Electronic Information* (Westport, Connecticut: Meckler Publishing, 1993). Unfortunately, this volume chiefly is characterized by its slim contents and its high price.

Brief Biographical Notes

IT IS NOT at all uncommon, of course, when you write a paper about some well-known figure of the past to have many references to other persons of the time in your work. Sometimes, it almost seems as if your litany of names is like the cast of a long-forgotten play or an old dusty novel. If this is the impression your whole text leaves with your reader, you have deadened your writing so much that even the most interested reader will lay aside your work with a yawn. One notable scholar has likened the pleasure he derived from reading such papers to the pleasure he derived from reading the telephone book. You must avoid the phenomenon of "telephone-book writing" at all costs. One way to do this, and, at the same time, preserve your reader's interest in the secondary people in your paper, is to place brief biographies of them in footnotes, when you mention them for the first time. More than one student has become fascinated with a historical figure or enthralled by a time in the past, not by reading a text about a major figure but by reading a footnote about a fascinating minor personage.

This principle is equally true for papers that are not, in the slightest degree, historical in their subjects or outlooks. In a paper on the evolution of chemical or physical processes or discoveries, when you may mention the names of persons living and working in their fields today, it is helpful to provide your reader with a brief note on the person's background and accomplishments, as well as a mention of where the person is working today. This last particular element often is called an "affiliation note," because you mention the organization with which the subject of your note is affiliated.

So, briefly identify persons of importance in your narrative who might be unknown to your reader. Indicate the time they lived and something of their accomplishments to set them into your narrative, without detracting from the main line of your discourse. For example, if you are discussing *Hamlet*, it is interesting to note that Shakespeare had a fascination with the form of this name, as shown by the fact that he named his only son

Hamnet, after the boy's godfather, Hamnet Sadler, more than fifteen years before he wrote the play. Hamnet is of no importance in discussing *Hamlet*, except as an illustration of Shakespeare's etymological bent.[1] You should not, of course, supply gratuitous biographical notes about people who are well known to your readers.

In the following example, written by a freshman for a survey course in English literature, the author's subject is the use of the name Titania for all sorts of purposes in the years since Shakespeare wrote *A Midsummer Night's Dream*. In the section of his paper from which our example is taken, he has no need to supply secondary information about either William Shakespeare or Carl Maria von Weber; but he does need to say something about both James Robinson Planché, who is forgotten today, and Christoph Martin Wieland, who, although still famous in Germany, is a figure of literature who is little appreciated by modern American readers.

1. The name also was spelled as Hamlet quite commonly in the sixteenth century. For a very brief discussion, see Oscar James Campbell, ed., *The Reader's Encyclopedia of Shakespeare* (New York: Thomas Y. Crowell Company, 1966) 751.

A student paper

Titania, with her connotation of airy grace and lightness, disappeared into the musical shadows during the eighteenth century. Perhaps there was no room for her in the elevated "Age of Reason." But she emerges, suddenly and magnificently, in the Romantic era in Carl Maria von Weber's opera, *Oberon*. This work, in three acts with an English text by James Robinson Planché,[1] is based much more extensively on Christoph Martin Wieland's[2]

1. James Robinson Planché was born February 27, 1796, in London. He was the son of a watchmaker with Huguenot antecedents. He became one of the leading playwrights in England in a generation little remembered for its contribution to the theatre. In addition, Planché was a theatrical manager and a well-known designer of theatrical costumes. In 1823, he designed the costumes for Charles Kemble's production of Shakespeare's *King John*, at Covent Garden. This was the first occasion on which the costumes were based on the historical dress of the time of the play's action, something which has now become virtually universal in theatre and film. Planché also became renowned as an antiquary and student of heraldry. In 1854, as a consequence of the great reputation he had made in the study of heraldry, he was appointed Rouge Croix pursuivant-of-arms; and, in 1866, he was advanced in the College of Heralds to the rank of Somerset Herald. He also is remembered for his *History of British Costumes*, published in 1834. He died in Chelsea on May 30, 1880. For additional details of his life and work, see his autobiography, *The Recollections and Reflections of J. R. Planché (Somerset Herald): A Professional Biography*, 2 vols. (London: Tinsley Brothers, 1872).

2. Christoph Martin Wieland (1733–1813) was, after Goethe and Schiller, perhaps the leading literary figure of the *sturm und drang* period in German literature. He composed "Oberon" between 1778 and 1780 and published it in the latter year. In about seven thousand lines, the poem combines the story of the quarrel between Oberon and Titania, as developed by Shakespeare, with the literarily larger story of Huon of Bordeaux. For additional details about the poem, see Henry and

poem, "Oberon," than it is on Shakespeare's play; and "Oberon" was, in turn, based on the medieval romance, *Huon de Bordeaux.*

Mary Garland, *The Oxford Companion to German Literature* (Oxford, Clarendon Press, 1976), 647–648; for biographical details on Wieland, see Derek Maurice Van Abbe, *Christoph Martin Wieland, 1733-1813: A Literary Biography* (London: Harrap, 1961).

In a second example from the same student's paper, we have chosen part of his discussion of the use of the name Titania in the titles of books. The author regards Gerald White Johnson's biography of Adolph Ochs as particularly noteworthy in this regard. In his note, he not only furnishes some useful biographical information about Ochs, but also provides a brief discussion of the biography itself. This footnote raises a part of the text, which would otherwise be lifeless, into an engaging moment for the reader. It must be remembered that neither Ochs nor Johnson's biography of him is germane to the topic of the paper, which is a discussion of the name Titania.

The use of Titania as an allusion in the titles of books is considerable. Two of these are worthy of notice. When Gerald White Johnson wrote his authorized biography of the American newspaper magnate, Adolph Simon Ochs, he entitled his work *An Honorable Titania: A Biographical Study of Adolph S. Ochs.*[1]

---

1. Ochs, who came from a Bavarian Jewish family, was born in Cincinnati, Ohio, on March 12, 1858. He, very early in life, embraced journalism. When only twenty years old, he took control of the Chattanooga, Tennessee, *Times*, and made it one of the leading daily journals in the South. In 1896, he acquired a controlling interest in the *New York Times*, and quickly made it one of the leading newspapers in the world. Defying the conventions of "yellow journalism," he set a new, high standard in American reportage. In 1925, he offered a subvention of $50,000 each year, for ten years, towards the issuance of the *Dictionary of American Biography*, for which he always will be remembered with kindness by scholars. By the time he died, in Chattanooga, on April 8, 1935, he had elevated the *New York Times* from a daily circulation of 9,000, in 1896, to 466,000.

Gerald White Johnson, who was born in 1889, published his life of Ochs in 1946. The first printing of *An Honorable Titania* bears the following imprint: New York: Harper & Brothers, 1946. It has nine introductory pages and three hundred thirteen pages of text, together with a frontispiece and a portrait of Ochs. The Library of Congress call number for this volume is: PN4874.O4J6.

Our next example of this type of note is taken from a term paper on the Mass of Bolsena that was written by a sophomore for a course in advanced expository writing. The paper was so well researched and well written that, with some revision and emendation, she published it within a few months after the conclusion of the course. That publication, in turn, attracted favorable comment in both the prestigious journal, *Science*,[2] and the British scientific magazine, *New Scientist*.[3]

The intention of her paper was to explore the question of whether or not a well-remembered miraculous occurrence in the thirteenth century, the appearance of blood on a host[4] during a Mass, could be explained, without prejudice to the original interpretation of the event, in terms of a series of microbiological events which recurred from time to time throughout history.

The portion of her narrative from which we excerpted a passage is a part of her introductory matter in which she reviews the essentials of the miracle itself and describes how other researchers had noticed similar phenomena in later centuries. She avoids the "telephone book" phenomenon of simply naming Bartolomeo Bizio, Vincenzo Sette, and Christian Gottfried Ehrenberg by providing brief biographical notes about them, which place them into the context of her paper.

2. "Miracle or Microbe?," *Science*, vol. 264 (13 May 1994) 903.
3. "The Miraculous Microbes of Bolsena," *New Scientist*, no. 1928 (4 June 1994) 14.
4. A wafer of sacramental bread.

Johanna C. Cullen, "The Microbiological Miracle of Bolsena,"
revised and published as "The Miracle of Bolsena," *ASM News*,
American Society for Microbiology, vol. 60, no. 4 (April 1994)
187–191

The purpose of this paper is not to challenge the
doctrine of transubstantiation, the miraculous nature of the Mass of Bolsena, nor the faith of the
priest, but to demonstrate that the physical mani-
festations during the miracle of the Mass of Bolsena
may have a more microbiological basis than a meta-
physical one. By reviewing the description of the
historical event of the Mass, other examples of
"bleeding" throughout history, and the relevant research conducted by Bartolomeo Bizio,[1] Vincenzo
Sette,[2] and Christian Gottfried Ehrenberg,[3] we can
see that the event in Bolsena may, in fact, have been
but a single link in a chain of events that began in
historical antiquity.

1. Bartolomeo Bizio was an Italian pharmacist who first attempted a natural explanation of the blood phenomenon. For
details, see Robert S. and Margaret E. Breed, "The Type Species
of the Genus Serratia, Commonly Known as *Bacillus prodigio-
sus*," *Journal of Bacteriology* 9 (1924) 548.

2. Vincenzo Sette was a physician and surgeon from Piove,
Italy, whose efforts towards a natural explanation for the blood
phenomenon paralleled those of Bizio. Sette's work, together
with that of Bizio, was of a "high order for the period in which
it was done." *Ibid.*

3. Christian Gottfried Ehrenberg (1795–1876) was a biolo-
gist, micropaleontologist, and a member of the Berlin Academy
of Sciences and of the Academie des Sciences of Paris. For additional details about his life and career, see Ilse Jahn, "Ehrenberg, Christian Gottfried," in Charles Coulston Gillespie, ed.,
Dictionary of Scientific Biography (New York: Charles Scribner's
Sons, 1981) 288–292. Although Ehrenberg's scientific work was
less complete than the earlier Italian work of Bizio and Sette,
he studied the history of the blood phenomenon much more
completely. See Breed and Breed, "Type Species of the Genus
Serratia," 552.

Sometimes, of course, there really is nothing to discover about the people you encounter in your research. No matter how hard you search, you cannot find any significant biographical details about them. Nevertheless, you should make some attempt to place them in the context of your writing. Perhaps the only material that you can find is from public or church records, or from a mention in someone else's letters or papers. Indeed, the latter case is quite often the way that these phantom persons of the past enter the writing of a modern student or scholar. If this is all that you have, by all means tell your reader that this is the case. If you can find more, perhaps in the same general source in which you found the person in the first place, then include that material to give some idea of flesh, blood, and time to the name you have just typed.

The following example is taken from a master's thesis that is an edition of a medieval English government document. The author first transcribed the account into modern Latin letters, and then extended the dozens of abbreviations in the original. Finally, after discussing the major figures who are mentioned in the account in his introduction, he tried to find out as much as he could about the minor figures whose names appear, almost incidentally, in the document. Two of them are John Frank and Nicholas Wymbish, both of whom were minor government clerks at the time the account was prepared. The reality of the lives of John and Nicholas remain hidden, probably forever, for they were simply not important enough to have had much written about them in their lifetimes, or shortly thereafter, or to have attracted the attention of scholars in later centuries. However, by searching through indices of the same general collection of documents from which the original account was taken, the author did discover their names in several other documents, some of which were grants to them. It is from this scanty material that he assembled his short biographical notes. They serve to place John and Nicholas in the context of both the document and the times in which they lived.[5]

5. Since the document is in Latin, we offer here a translation of the text that appears in the example: "The account of John Radecliffe, knight, once constable of Bordeaux, by writ of the lord Henry V, once the king of England, fa-

ther of the present lord king, under his great seal dated the sixteenth day of May in the seventh year of his reign, enrolled in a certain roll by John Frank, the clerk of the rolls of the chancery of the lord king, delivered here at the exchequer of account of the lord king, at the hands of Nicholas Wymbyssh, clerk; delivered and remaining with these particulars; in which, among other things, it is contained that the same former king fully confident of the faithfulness and circumspection of the aforesaid John has granted to the same John the aforesaid office to be held, occupied, and exercised by himself or his sufficient deputies for whom he was prepared to respond so long as it pleased the same former king."

A master's thesis

Compotus Johannis Radeclyff militis nuper con-
stabularii Burdegale per breve domini Henrici
quinti nuper regis Anglie patris domini regis nunc
de magno sigillo suo dat' 16 die Maii anno regni sui
7 irrotulatum in quodam rotulo per Johannem
Frank[1] clericum rotulorum cancellarie domini regis
per manus Nicholai Wymbyssh[2] clerici hic ad scac-
carium domini regis de recordo liberatum et penes
has particulas remanens in quo inter cetera con-
tinetur quod idem nuper rex de fidelitate et cir-
cumspeccione predicti Johannis plenius confidens
concessit eidem Johanni officium predictum haben-
dum, occupandum et exercendum per se vel suffi-
cientes deputatos suos pro quibus respondere vel-
let quamdiu eidem nuper regi placeret . . .

1. John Frank appears often in the calendars of various
classes of royal documents. As early as July 4, 1393, he was
granted the sum of 6d. daily for life (*Calendar of Patent Rolls
1399–1401* [hereafter *C. P. R.*], m. 12, November 14, 1399)
and, in addition, he is mentioned as being the master or warden of the house or hospital of St. John the Baptist, Hungerford, and parson or warden of the free chapel of Staundon by
Hungerford (*C. P. R. 1399–1401*, m. 34, October 14, 1399), as
well as being the holder of the prebendaries of Tyderyngton
and Hornyngesham in the collegiate church of Heghtredebury,
in the diocese of Salisbury, and of Wylmecote in the collegiate
church or chapel of Tameworth, in the diocese of Coventry and
Lichfield (*C .P. R. 1413–1416*, m. 33, October 16, 1415).
2. This Nicholas Wymbyssh, or Wymbish, was the cousin of
Eleanor Cobham, later wife of Humphrey Plantagenet, Duke of
Gloucester. He is mentioned several times in the *Calendar of
Patent Rolls* among them as having been presented with the
church of Pery alias Poterespery, in the diocese of Lincoln (*C.
P. R. 1413–1416*, m. 20, June 18, 1414). *Cf.* E. F. Jacob, *The Fifteenth Century: 1399–1485* (Oxford: Clarendon Press, 1961)
485.

Geographical Identification

THE WORLD is filled with hundreds of thousands of named locations—cities, towns, rivers, mountains, deserts, gardens, palaces, office buildings, and cemeteries, to mention only a few. Not even the best educated reader will be familiar with more than a small percentage of them.

You should add a note to describe and locate places that are strange or unfamiliar to your reader, so that she may follow your writing with a heightened understanding of the geography in which your text moves.

Of special importance are those cases where the names of towns, cities, and natural features have been changed, which obliges you to make your reader fully aware of these changes. For example, how many people will know that Sankt Peterbourg was Leningrad during most of the twentieth century—two hundred years from now.

If you do not take the time to identify the names of unfamiliar places for your reader, she simply will be looking at a list of words—devoid of a sense of place, color, time, and human association.

An example of the use of the footnote to identify a geographical site which may not be well known to the reader comes from an undergraduate paper which reviews the geography used by Henry James to add verisimiltude to his novella, *Daisy Miller*. In this paper, "Alone! The Roman Experience of Daisy Miller," the student has reached the point where Daisy has been buried in the Protestant Cemetery in Rome and he needs to say something about this landmark, without detracting from the main thread of his narrative. Two points are worthy of special notice in this note. First, the student uses the last lines of the footnote to thank the person who originally suggested his sources to him; and, second, he incorporates interior citations to works which provide additional information on the subject of the note. This is a valuable technique, which allows the writer to point the reader to interesting material which lies outside the scope of the paper itself.

In the epilogue to the tragedy of Daisy Miller, Daisy herself has one more chance to communicate with the reader through her mother's recital of her last message to Winterbourne. Daisy wishes Frederick to know that she was never engaged to Giovanelli and that she hopes he remembers their visit to the Castle of Chillon. The first part of the message is Daisy's attempt to rehabilitate herself in Frederick's eyes; the second is her touching upon an earlier moment when she was not isolated and alienated from the society around her. In little more than a week after Frederick receives Daisy's last message, he is standing at the side of her grave in the Protestant Cemetery in Rome.[1]

1. The Protestant Cemetery was established in the reign of Clement XII [Lorenzo Corsini, 1730–1740] to meet the immediate needs of the foreign diplomatic community in Rome. The oldest extant grave dates from 1738. The Cemetery is divided into two sections. The older of the two was closed in 1825, having become full. It is in this section that the bodies of John Keats [died February 23, 1821] and his friend, Joseph Severn [died August 3, 1879] are to be found. Severn's body was interred beside that of Keats as a tribute to their friendship, in spite of the fact that the older section of the cemetery had been closed for more than half a century. Severn's grave is the newest, therefore, in the old section. Of this part of the Cemetery, Shelley wrote, in his preface to "Adonais": "The cemetery is an open space among the ruins, covered in winter with violets and *daisies* [italics mine]. It might make one in love with death, to think that one should be buried in so sweet a place." (Percy Bysshe Shelley, "Adonais," in *John Keats and Percy Bysshe Shelley: Complete Poetical Works*. New York: The Modern Library, n. d., p. 484).

The newer section was opened in 1825. One of he earliest interments there was of the heart of Shelley, who had drowned in the Gulf of Spezia on July 8, 1822. Shelley's body was not recovered until August 16, and, by then, the remains were in such condition that they were cremated on the beach of the Gulf, under the care of his friend, Edward John Trelawny. Later, Trelawny brought Shelley's heart to be buried in the Protestant Cemetery. Many years later, when Trelawny himself died, at Sompting, near Worthing in Sussex, on August 13, 1881, his remains also were cremated and taken to Rome for interment beside Shelley's heart.

Many other figures of note in the nineteenth century are buried in the newer section of the Cemetery, including John Addington Symonds, the distinguished historian [died April 19, 1893], and August Goethe, the son of Johann Wolfgang von Goethe [died 1830]. For additional details and mentions of other persons who are buried here, see Augustus J. C. Hare, *Walks in Rome*, fifteenth edition revised (New York: George Routledge & Sons, n. d.), pp. 696–698; Karl Baedeker, *Central Italy and Rome: Handbook for Travellers*, fifteenth revised edition (Leipzig: Karl Baedeker, Publisher, 1909) p. 329; and Stuart Rossiter, *The Blue Guides: Rome and Environs*, edited by Alta Macadam (London: Ernest Benn Limited, 1975), pp. 87–88.

I thank Dr. Michelangelo Tanara for his assistance in helping me to gather materials on the Protestant Cemetery, and particularly for help me to verify the dates of the deaths of the persons mentioned above.

In our second example, from a doctoral dissertation on the translations from German poetry done by the American poet, James Wright (1927–1980), in his youth, the author refers to one of Wright's last poems to show how the poetic developments which began in his youth reached their fruition at the end of his life. The setting of this poem is the small Italian village of Anghiari, which was, in the fifteenth century, the site of a major battle in the wars of the Italian city states. Of course, the place is of little concern to the author, who is analysing the work as a reflection of Wright's poetic purpose. But, she knows that it will be helpful to her reader's understanding of Wright's inspiration to provide information which places Wright himself in the geography that moved the poet to write the poem. She does this with a short note that explains both the location of the town in northern Italy and its historical significance, of which Wright was well aware. In the note, she provides several references to major figures of the Italian Renaissance, which can act as starting point for the reader who wishes to know more about the town and its place in history.

A doctoral dissertation

In *This Journey* (1982), the poem, "The Journey," describes the final stage of Wright's quest where he
discovers, at the site of Florence's great defence of
her liberty,[1] the secret for which he has been
searching, the acceptance of death and of life on
their own terms:

> Anghiari is medieval, a sleeve sloping down
> A steep hill, suddenly sweeping out
> To the edge of a cliff, and dwindling.
> But far up the mountain, behind the town,
> We too were swept out, out by the wind,
> Alone with the Tuscan grass.
>
> Wind had been blowing across the hills
> For days, and everything now was graying gold
> With dust, everything we saw, even
> Some small children scampering along a road,
> Twittering Italian to a small caged bird.
> We sat beside them to rest in some brushwood,
> And I leaned down to rinse the dust from my face.

1. The battle of Anghiari, now remembered only by persons
who have a political philosophy which praises both political
freedom and individual liberty, was fought on June 29, 1440, between the forces of Florence, and her ally, Venice, under the
command of Francesco Sforza, and Milanese forces led by Nic-
colo Piccinino. The Florentine victory was later regarded by
the citizens of the Republic as the signal salvation of their liberty. Later, the great, and now lost, mural by Leonardo da Vinci
in the Palazzo Signoria commemorated this battle.

This type of footnote also is valuable for providing detailed descriptions of small geographical entities to help your reader to understand not only the size and placement of a site in relation to its surroundings but also something of its detailed appearance and use, past or present.

In our final example, from an anthropological work on the Vedda people of India that is still respected, in spite of its age, for the wealth of data recorded, we see a footnote which not only serves the need discussed above but also modifies and amplifies the original detail presented in the text, because of new information.

The Seligmanns begin their work with a description of the historical and geographical background of the Veddas, placing them broadly in the context of their environment and in the context of the antiquity of their culture. In establishing the great age of Vedda culture, the authors describe a number of archaeological excavations, based upon letters that they received from the excavators, including James Parsons, Director of the Mineral Survey of India, who died before he could provide a fuller account of his work. Later, the Seligmanns received a more detailed letter from the owner of the property on which Parsons discovered the ancient cave. The second letter, with its amplification of detail, is the subject of their footnote.

C[harles] G[abriel] Seligmann and Brenda Z. Seligmann, *The Veddas* (Cambridge: Cambridge University Press, 1911) 20–22

Within the last few months the range of these implements has been extended south to the neighborhood of Ratnapura, where a number of excellent specimens were found by the late James Parsons, who wrote to us concerning them as follows: "I dug out a cave in Sabaragamuwa in a ravine to the northeast of Ratnapura which was most interesting. I have full notes of the cave—briefly it is sufficiently high above the stream for it to have been impossible for it to enter the cave in geologically recent times. To a depth of 8 feet the cave is full of black earth containing many shells of the big tree snail mixed with the river shells, *bellan* (*Paludina ceylonica*), in such abundance that these shells are now occasionally collected and burnt for chunam. A shell is said to occur that is found only in the river Ratnapura, but I did not succeed in finding it. The tradition is that the molluscs were used as food by 'an ancient Tamil people.' The shells are not calcined, but with them were a number of flakes of clear quartz—mostly made from pebbles, some of them the best I have seen and undoubtedly neolithic. . . . I do not think there can be any reasonable doubt about them. At a depth of five feet very rotten fragments of the top of a human skull and the region of the ear besides bits of long bones and some pieces of chert not obviously worked. At the entrance of the cave there is a sort of dyke thrown up, which is full of flakes some of which appear to be ground and polished."

Parsons' premature death renders it unlikely that a full account of this find will ever be published, but owing to the kindness of Mrs Parsons we have been able to examine a number of the implements excavated by her husband. These include a number of cores, worked flakes and scrapers, and one flake of chert showing a bulb of percussion, but none of the specimens that I have handled show any signs of polishing.[1]

1. Since the above was written we have received the following account of the cave from Mr W. D. Holland on whose property we understand the cave is situated. "The cave is situated about a mile from my bungalow on the N. bank of a small stream and some 10 to 15 feet above present water level. The cave has been formed by the weathering out of a soft core of rock from gneiss of the ordinary kind and may have been assisted by the action of the stream when running at a higher level. The cave is a fairly large one and would accommodate several families, say 15 or 20 individuals, and is quite dry inside. It appears to have been banked up in front, but this may have been caused by debris falling from the cliff above. The strike I believe coincides with the stream S.W. N.W. We dug a pit about 5 feet in diameter and about 7 or 8 feet deep, and came upon a lot of shells of the belan or water snail and some bones: a much shattered portion of the latter we thought to be a portion of a human skull, and Mr Parsons subsequently informed me by letter that this had been confirmed in Colombo. . . . The quartz flakes were not found in the cave, but on the entrance bank where they had been exposed by the drip from the rock above washing the earth away and leaving them. The old inhabitants would naturally work at the entrance for the sake of light. I know only of this one cave in this neighbourhood. The stream flows S.W. to the Kaluganga (eventually), and rises about 1½ miles (bee line) to the east in the range which forms the watershed of the Kaluganga and Wallawe rivers. The elevation is approximately 1900 feet and the cave faces S. (about). The Sinhalese have used this cave for a mine for the shells of the belan, which they burn into lime to eat with betel leaf. A large number of shells must have been removed but notwithstanding there must still be an enormous quantity left. We were also informed by the natives that there are two kinds of belan shells found in the cave, only one of which is found in the neighbouring streams and the other must have been brought from some distance in the Ratnapura direction, 15 or 20 miles, and they inferred that these had been brought by whoever had lived in the cave, presumably for food. We also found some fragments of

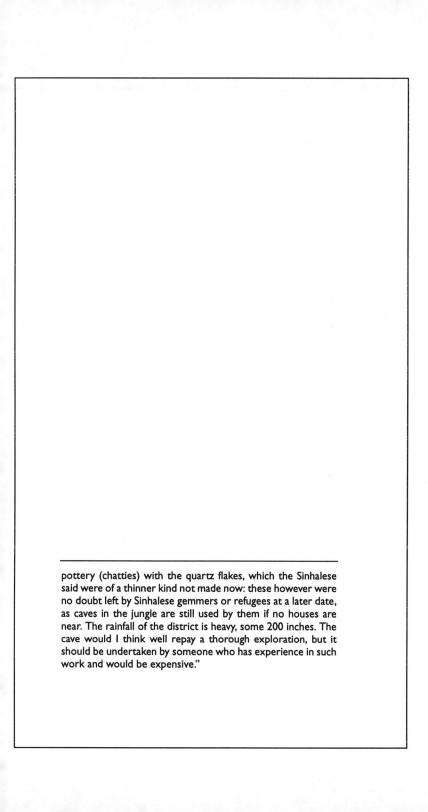

pottery (chatties) with the quartz flakes, which the Sinhalese said were of a thinner kind not made now: these however were no doubt left by Sinhalese gemmers or refugees at a later date, as caves in the jungle are still used by them if no houses are near. The rainfall of the district is heavy, some 200 inches. The cave would I think well repay a thorough exploration, but it should be undertaken by someone who has experience in such work and would be expensive."

Using Footnotes to Describe Objects

USE A FOOTNOTE to describe physically any object which your reader must be able to visualize. Even if you provide an illustration in the text or in an appendix, your reader may not really comprehend the size or scope of the object.[1] You may, for example, have an occasion to mention some device from the past and note its purpose, yet your reader may not be able to visualize with clarity the object you describe—not just the physical dimensions but also the placement of the object in its surroundings, especially with regard to its use. For example, almost everyone, at least in film, has seen hames. Yet how many people can be expected to know, with any real precision, what the device was or how it was used.[2]

Likewise, you can use this kind of footnote to identify esoteric occupations and the devices or mechanisms associated with them. For instance, one of the most highy skilled, and highly paid, workmen in the world is the traditonal *degorgeur*, yet hardly anyone really understands what he does.[3] If you were describing the process by which genuine champagne is made, you would use a footnote to describe his job. By the same token you will need a footnote if, during a discussion of electrical locomotives, you mention the pantograph. Your reader may well wonder why a device to duplicate handwriting or tracing is to be

1. This is the principal reason that archeological photographs, and some others, as well, always have a scale or rule placed within the image itself. Earlier, photographers would place people in the photograph just for the purpose of showing a relative scale, as is the case with so many illustrative photographs of monuments in Egypt that were taken in the last century.

2. The hame was the collar placed over the neck of a draught animal. Since daught animals often worked in teams, hames, in the form of a cojoined pair, also were common. The devices frequently were gilded or ornamented elaborately—often to a degree that they could be called works of art. Generally, hames were secured to the animal with leather straps, which were, in some cases, passed back through the upper part of the collar and backward to the driver's hands, thus forming reins. The American surname "Haymaker" derives not from someone who made hay but, rather, from the German word "hammacher," one who made hames.

3. In the traditional process of making champagne, in which all fermentation takes place in the bottle, each bottle gradually is turned from its original

found on such a locomotive. Of course, *your* pantograph is something quite other than *your reader's* pantograph.[4]

In creating this type of note, make sure that the units in which you express the dimensions of an object are, themselves, clear and comprehensible to your reader. Do not give figures for which you do not supply the unit of reference. To say that something has a length and width of ".603 x .345" means nothing, if your reader cannot tell if you mean centimeters or meters, inches or feet, or some other unit.

Our first example is from a freshman term paper on Gerard Dou's painting, *The Hermit,* now in the collection of the National Gallery of Art in Washington, D.C. The author thinks that it will help his readers to know how the painting is framed, yet that certainly is not a part of his discussion of the painting itself, and its history. Consequently, he creates a footnoted text to allow his readers to see the work in its physical context today.

---

upright position until it is inverted in a special rack, called a *pupitre*; then, when it is completely upside down, *mise sur pointe*, the *degorgeur* pulls the cork from each bottle with great precision; the remaining yeast cells and the sediment are fired from the bottle at high pressure, after which the degorgeur reinserts the cork, very quickly indeed, after which it is wired down. Over the space of some weeks, each bottle is returned to its upright position gradually. For a brief description of this process, see Alexis Lichine, *Alexis Lichine's New Encyclopedia of Wines & Spirits,* rev. and enlarged (New York: Alfred A. Knopf, 1978) 159–161.

4. The pantograph on an electric locomotive is that mechanism on a collapsible frame which is raised from the roof of the engine to touch the power lines above. It is through the pantograph that electric power is conveyed from the lines to the motors. Perhaps the most famous engines with pantographs in the history of American railroading were the great GG-1 class of engines, built by General Electric for the Pennsylvania Railroad and used for many years on the electrified lines from Washington, D. C., to New York City, and from Philadelphia to Harrisburg, Pennsylvania. For a discussion of the pantograph and its use in transmitting electricity, see Joseph Voris Lamson, *Contact Line Wear Control on Heavy Electric Traction Systems Using the Pantograph Type of Slider Current Collectors* (Seattle, Washington: University of Washington, 1935). For a description of the GG-1 and its fame in American railroad history, see Frederic H. Abendschein, *Career of a Champion: The Story of the First GG1* (Quarryville, Pennsylvania: Lancaster Chapter, NRHS [National Railway Historical Society], 1984). A fine, twenty-nine-minute film that traces the history and fame of the GG-1 is *GG-1: An American Classic* (Verona, New Jersey: Avanti Productions, 1984).

Dou's paintings of hermits and Magdalens fall into the genre of *Vanitas*. They represented a getaway to a moment of seclusion, in which one could reflect quietly on life's brevity—indicated by the recurring images of the extinguished lamp, the dead tree, the Bible, the human skull, and the hourglass. Dou's paintings do, however, also hold out the promise of a new life after death, shown in the image of young grass and new leaves springing from the dead trees.

One can gain more insight into Dou's treatment of religious themes in general, and hermits in particular, by examining carefully, and in detail, one example from his work in this *genre*. If a single painting is to be considered, a good candidate is *The Hermit*, which is now in the collection of the National Gallery of Art in Washington, D.C. It arrived there from the Timken Collection on March 15, 1960.[1]

1. The National Gallery's receipt number for the painting is 2103. The size of the cradled panel is 18 1/8 inches high by 13 5/8 inches wide. The "ornate rectangular frame, [with] gold leaf over gesso and red bole, [has an] arched opening for the painting." The frame is a majestic piece, in itself. It is 23¾ inches high by 19¾ inches wide. The gesso and red bole which are built onto the wood are, respectively, a gypsum-based plaster, similar to plaster of fine, and a compound of fine, compact, earthy, unctuous clay that has been made red by the presence of a heavy infusion of iron oxide. The base of the frame's construction is of two pieces of oak. The main piece is bentwood, with an arched section above. The secondary section is a cut rectangular piece fastened below the main section. The two pieces were fastened together with glue, which was revealed by a modern x-radiographic analysis. It showed traces of the glue in one of the corners. The rectangular piece seems to have been added at a later date, "probably to fit a frame for which it was not originally intended." For further details, see the *Provenence*

File for this painting, National Gallery of Art, Washington, D.C., page 2.

Of course, the object you describe need not be limited to a small artifact. Sometimes, objects such as buildings and other large entities are worthy subjects for this type of note. Even if you include illustrations or diagrams, a careful description in prose may help your reader to place the structure in the context of its landscape—by providing dimensions and some indication of purpose.

Our next example is far from the size of the frame of a painting. It is taken from one of the principal manuals to Classical Greek architecture to have been written in the past half century. The author begins by describing the salient features of early Greek buildings of the Neolithic Age and the Early Bronze Age. He then moves swiftly to a consideration of early Minoan architecture, with a discussion of the early Cretan palaces of Middle Minoan I and Middle Minoan II. Notice here that his discourse is concerned with the generalities of his subject, and not with particular buildings or purposes. If he were to break the flow of his narrative with a long consideration of the nature and function of one building, he would sacrifice, in all probability, the concentration of his reader; hence the note.

A[rnold] W[alter] Lawrence, *Greek Architecture*, 2d ed. (Harmondsworth, Middlesex: Penguin Books, Ltd., 1967) 24

Of these palaces Mallia alone gives any appearance of having been defensive, and that merely by chance. At Cnossus and Phaestus in this period, and in all subsequent Minoan palaces, the planning shows clearly that no thought of defensibility entered the minds of those responsible for the layout. Furthermore, the Minoan towns were absolutely indefensible, and even in the countryside, well adapted to brigandage as it is, no vestige of Minoan fortification has been identified.[1]

1. The supposed block-houses or police-posts in the countryside might, for all one can tell, have been inns, or served some equally innocuous purpose. A doubtful exception should perhaps be made for a building of Middle Minoan I at Khamaizi (J[ohn] D[evitt] S[tringfellow] Pendlebury, *Archaeology of Crete: An Introduction* [London: Methuen & Co., Ltd., 1939,] p. 100, figure 14; Donald Struan Robertson, *A Handbook of Greek and Roman Architecture*, 2d ed. [Cambridge: Cambridge University Press, 1929], figure 1). The exterior is oval, 73 by 48 feet maximum. The shape was obviously adopted to make the most of a site restricted by nature, and the customary rectangular planning was modified as little as possible; most of the partitions are set at right angles, making the rooms rectangular except where they utilize a stretch of the outer wall. An empty space in the centre presumably formed a diminutive court; it contains the well-head of a cistern. At the entrance, one wall radiates towards it, converging upon the other, which runs at right angles to the exterior; this inward narrowing of the porch could have been intended as a safeguard against attack (supposing that the porch had no roof, which seems improbable). The external wall is badly built and little more than 3 feet thick, a proof that the building was not strictly a fort.

The descriptive footnote can be concerned with function as well as form. Indeed, many readers may be able to visualize an object or mechanism without having a clear idea of how that entity functions. Yet, in a closely reasoned essay, the author may need to ensure that her reader does understand the operative nature of something, before she can proceed to a consideration of its general effect.

In *Revolution in Time*, David S. Landes sets out to show how a concern for the accurate measurement of time was one of the leading ideas which shaped the modern world. In the evolution of the idea of the perfection of timekeeping, the development of the pendulum was a major event. Before he continues with the principal thread of his discourse, he needs to explain to his readers why this is so. But once he has shown that a common pendulum must swing in a cycloidal arc in order to be useful as a timekeeper, he does not wish to digress further by discussing the mathematical properties of cycloids. At the same time, however, he needs to offer his more interested readers some discussion of this, to lay the groundwork for the discussion that is to follow. He fills this need by supplying a footnote, which offers all the necessary information for those who want it without any interruption to the flow of his discourse.[5]

David S. Landes, *Revolution in Time: Clocks and the Making of the Modern World* (Cambridge, Massachusetts: The Belknap Press of Harvard University Press, 1983) 118–119

The new timekeeper seems simple and obvious from the vantage of hindsight. At the time, though, the use of the pendulum posed some interesting difficulties. Two in particular are worth noting here, the first because it shows the paradoxical advantage of a little ignorance; the second, because it further exemplifies the law of error. The responses to both illustrate the technological version of the economist's derived demand: innovation begets innovation.

As to the first: Galileo thought that the oscillation of a pendulum is independent of the amplitude of swing; that only the length (the radius of the arc) matters. This is one reason why he thought the pendulum could serve as or in a *misuratore del tempo*. When he found that this was not true, he attributed the variance to air resistance. He was right about that: air resistance does make a difference. But it is a very small difference, and it was not to matter for another two hundred fifty years, when the ever increasing fineness of astronomical observations and the invention of better pumps made it worthwhile and feasible to put observatory regulators into vacuum chambers. The major source of the difficulty was the arc of oscillation: a pendulum weight swinging from a point describes a circle, and circular swings are not isochronous. To obtain isochronism, a *cycloidal* arc is required — circle rolling along a straight line. This is because the common cycloid (a very uncommon curve!) is a tautochrone (from the Greek *tautos*, the same, and *chronos*, time), which means that a ball or bead or pendulum bob starting anywhere along the curve and impelled only by the force of gravity will reach the bottom in the same time. This is not the kind of result that one would expect intuitively, but a little thought will explain why. The higher one starts along the curve, the greater the velocity of the falling object, and this increased speed makes up for the longer distance traversed.

This deviation of the circular pendulum from the isochronism of the cycloid is what the horologist calls *circular error*.[1] For very small arcs, where the two curves almost coincide, the difference is negligible, but it increases with the amplitude of oscillation. An increase of amplitude from one to two degrees of semiarc adds 4.95 seconds to a clock's daily rate, whereas an increase from five to six degrees adds 18.09 seconds. Huygens, applying the pendulum to verge-escapement bracket clocks, very quickly became aware of this error, for a simple reason: verge clocks, in order to work, required an oscillation of the pallet arbor (the verge itself) of wide amplitude, yielding pendulum swings of twenty degrees and more.

1. The circular pendulum swings slower: (1) because, for a given radius (length of rod), the arc traversed by a cycloidal pendulum is shorter (in geometric terms, the base of the cycloid is shorter than the chord subtending the circular arc of swing, and the cycloidal curve lies entirely within the segment defined by that chord and arc); and (2) because the common cycloid is brachistochronous (from *brachistos*, meaning the shortest, and *chronos*, time) — that is, it is the fastest path for an object falling from a higher point to a lower one not in the same vertical line. Here again the result goes against intuition, which would expect the fastest path to be the straight line connecting the two points, if only because it is the shortest distance. This time the greater velocity imparted by the steeper fall at the start of the drop more than makes up for the longer

traverse, indeed minimizes the time required. Anything shallower would not move the falling or rolling object fast enough; anything deeper would make it cover too long a path. In practical-fantastic terms: if a contestant in the soap-box auto derby could somehow persuade the organizers to let him run his car in a cycloidal chute, he would beat all the rest — assuming that his vehicle was no worse than the others.

The proof of the brachistochronism of the cycloid was found in 1696, in response to a challenge by Johann Bernoulli to "the sharpest mathematicians in the world." Bernoulli gave the contestants six months to solve the problem. Leibniz solved it the day he received it. What is more, he correctly predicted that only five persons would solve it and named them: himself, Newton, the two brothers Bernoulli, and Guillaume de l'Hospital, who needed some help from Bernoulli in the process. (Is there any other field in which the order of excellence [power] is so accurately known as in mathematics?) Jakob Bernoulli's solution, though not so ingenious and elegant as that of his younger brother and rival, anticipated the development of a new branch of mathematics, the calculus of variations. Charles C. Gillispie, ed., *Dictionary of Scientific Biography*, vol. 2 (New York: Scribner's, 1970), s.v. "Johann Bernoulli," p. 53.

Expanding Information
on a Secondary Topic

USE A FOOTNOTE to refer your reader to more detailed sources of information about an important, but secondary, topic in your essay, especially when that topic is not central to the main thesis of your paper but may be of considerable interest in its own right.

Our first example of this type of note is taken from John Bagnell Bury's edition of Edward Gibbon's great historical classic, *The Decline and Fall of the Roman Empire*. In the text itself, Gibbon discusses the chaos in the medieval German empire after the death of Frederick II in 1250. After his introductory summary of the political conditions of the time, Gibbon turns to describe the method by which the emperors were elected. In that passage, he merely lists the official positions of the seven electors, but Bury, in a well-placed note, offers additional detail and refers the reader to another source, from which he quotes, which has a modern scholarly, and itself famous, discussion of the process of the imperial election—Viscount Bryce's *The Holy Roman Empire*.[1]

1. James Bryce, *The Holy Roman Empire*, new ed. (London: Macmillan & Co., Ltd., 1904).

Edward Gibbon, *The History of the Decline and Fall of the
Roman Empire*, ed. J[ohn] B[agnell] Bury, 7 vols. (London:
Methuen & Co., Ltd., 1911) V:326–327.

After the death of Frederic the Second, Germany was left a monster with a hundred heads. A
crowd of princes and prelates disputed the ruins of
the empire; the lords of innumerable castles were
less prone to obey than to imitate their superiors;
and, according to the measure of their strength,
their incessant hostilities received the names of
conquest or robbery. Such anarchy was the inevitable consequence of the laws and manners of
Europe; and the kingdoms of France and Italy were
shivered into fragments by the violence of the same
tempest. But the Italian cities and French vassals
were divided and destroyed, while the union of the
Germans has produced, under the name of an empire, a great system of federative republic. In the
frequent and at last the perpetual institution of
diets, a national spirit was kept alive, and the powers of a common legislature are still exercised by
the three branches or colleges of the electors, the
princes, and the free and Imperial cities of Germany. I. Seven of the most powerful feudatories
were permitted to assume, with a distinguished
name and rank, the exclusive privilege of choosing
the Roman emperor; and these electors were the
king of Bohemia, the duke of Saxony, the margrave
of Brandenburg, the count palatine of the Rhine,
and the three archbishops of Metz, of Treves, and
of Cologne.[1]

1. The electoral college "is mentioned A.D. 1152, and in
somewhat clearer terms in 1198, as a distinct body; but without anything to show who composed it. First in A.D. 1263 does
a letter of Pope Urban IV. say that by immemorial custom the

right of choosing the Roman king belonged to seven persons, the seven who had just divided their votes on Richard of Cornwall and Alphonso of Castile." The three archbishops represented the German church; the four lay electors should have been the four great dukes of Saxony, Franconia, Bavaria, and Swabia. But the duchies of Franconia (or East Francia) and Swabia were extinct, their place being taken by the Palatinate of the Rhine and the Margraviate of Brandenburg. A conflict for the seventh place between Bavaria and the king of Bohemia (who claimed it by virtue of his office of cup-bearer) was decided by the Emperor Rudolf in 1289 in favor of the king of Bohemia (Bryce, *Holy Roman Empire* (ed. 1904), p. 238–9.)

Another example of the use of a footnote to expand information that is only touched upon in the main body of the text comes from a formal book review by an undergraduate at the University of Maryland entitled "A Review Of Thomas Carlyle's Last Book: *The Early Kings Of Norway.*"

After giving some critical examples of Carlyle's diction, the author indicates that these examples are, themselves, condensed from Carlyle's principal source, a major work of the saga tradition.

In the note, the student not only offers evidence on which translation of the *Heimskringla* actually was used by Carlyle as his source—for he could not read any of the ancient or modern Scandinavian languages—but also presents several modern editions of the great classic history of the Vikings, from the scholarly to the popular. In this way, the student reaches a varied audience whose interest in the older text may exist on different levels of education and understanding.

A student paper

These examples of Carlyle's conversational diction reveal what is perhaps the most winning quality of the book for the casual reader. Also, in this way, Carlyle simplifies the complex stories that are to be found in his principal source, the *Heimskringla* of Snorre Sturluson,[1] and adds a value of entertainment to the text.

1. The *Heimskringla* is a chain of sagas written in the early thirteenth century by Snorre Sturluson (1179–22/23 September 1241), an Icelandic magistrate who was close to the Norwegian king Håkon Håkonsson den Gamle (1217–1263). The sagas cover a period from the legendary Yngling kings to the victory of King Magnus Erlingsson over the Birkebeiner at the battle of Re in January, 1177. For biographical details on Snorre Sturluson, see Marlene Ciklamini, *Snorri Sturluson*, Twayne's World Authors Series; TWAS 493 (Boston: Twayne Publishers, 1978).

The translation that Carlyle used as his source is Snorri Sturluson, *The Heimskringla; or, Chronicle of The Kings of Norway*, trans. Samuel Laing, 3 vols. (London: Longman, Brown, Green, and Longmans, 1844). This is proven by the extensive number of quotations included in Carlyle's book which are direct transcriptions of the text of the Laing translation.

Today, the standard scholarly edition of the sagas is Snorri Sturluson, *Heimskringla*, ed. Bjarni Aðalbjarnarson. 3 vols, Islenzk Fornrit, vols. XXVI–XXVIII (Reykjavík: Hið Íslenzka Fornritfélag, 1941–1945). Two later translations of the *Heimskringla* into English are of considerable importance. The older, and more romantically styled, is Snorri Sturluson, *The Stories of the Kings of Norway, called the Round World (Heimskringla)*, 4 vols., trans. William Morris and Eiríkr Magnússon, The Saga Library, vols. III–VI, eds. William Morris and Eiríkr Magnússon (London: Bernard Quaritch, 1893–1905). The more recent, blander, and more faithful is Snorre Sturlason, *Heimskringla, or the Lives of the Norse Kings*, trans. Erling Monsen, with the assistance of A. H. Smith (Cambridge: W. Heffer & Sons, Ltd., 1932; repr. New York: Dover Publications, Inc., 1990).

The best popular modern Scandinavian edition is *Snorre Sturluson, Norges Kongesagaer*, eds. Finn Hødnebø and Hallvard

Magerøy, trans. Anne Holtsmark and Didrik Arup Seip (Oslo: Gyldendal Norsk Forlag A[ksjer]/S[elskap], Den Norske Bokklubben, 1981).

Glossing Unusual Words or Expressions

USE A FOOTNOTE to define, and perhaps to illustrate with examples, words, phrases, or expressions with which you are quite certain that your reader is unfamiliar. This note is not just for jargon, but also for words that you use in unusual ways or terms which may be confusing to your reader, because they have several different, but quite close, meanings.

You must remember that the English language today has a vocabulary of nearly seven hundred thousand words. No reader, no matter how well-educated or informed, can know more than a fraction of the words that are available to you, the writer. Because this is true, any word that you expect to be beyond the knowledge of the generally well-informed reader deserves a footnote, to ensure that your reader grasps fully your intention in choosing the word.

You can use this type of footnote to comment on common words or expressions which you find particularly interesting, perhaps in a special context, and which you think your reader will, too.

This type of note is quite separate from the notes that you use to gloss or translate words or expressions from foreign languages. These will be discussed elsewhere.

The following example is taken from John Livingston Lowes's masterful work on Samuel Taylor Coleridge, *The Road to Xanadu*.

John Livingston Lowes, *The Road to Xanadu: A Study in the Ways of the Imagination* (Boston: Houghton Mifflin Company, 1927) 313

I have tried more than once—as who that has read them has not?—to capture the secret of the charm which the old travellers by land and sea somehow communicated to their style. Does it not lie, after all (we ask ourselves), in those engaging idiosyncrasies of speech, with their pungently individual flavour, which strew the pages of the travel-books, as Marten's captivating 'Rose-like-shaped Slime-fish' strewed the sea, 'numerous as Atomes in the Air'? We read, and lay the book aside, and go about our business, and it is ten to one that the relish of some artlessly piquant turn of phrase lingers happily on our palate. The sharp tang of the style has the freshness of the salt smell of the sea.[1]

1. Since this is a chapter on diction, it is incumbent upon me, in view of this sentence, to say a word for 'tang.' In a sorely needed and characteristically delightful article in the *Atlantic Monthly* (August, 1924), Miss Repplier thus stigmatizes 'tang': 'a bit of educated slang worse than the slang of the gutters' (p. 185). That is a scathing indictment, and it is not without warrant. But (and this I am bound to insist) the fact that a word is mercilessly abused may not be permitted to debar its proper use—else we must face, in these slack days, an intolerable impoverishment of our inherited vocabulary. Few Englishmen have written more pure, perspicuous, racy, and idiomatic English than Thomas Gray, and when I read, for example, in his letters: 'The language has a tang of Shakespeare,' I decline to let the slang of the day dispossess me of my inheritance. When 'tang,' or any other great (or little) injured word, says precisely what we mean to say, it is still indefeasibly ours to use. I need scarcely add that I am defending a principle, and not a particular case which has no slightest interest to anybody but myself.

'Colourful,' by the way, which Miss Repplier pillories with 'tang,' is in a totally different category, and has no leg to stand on in any court. Spawned in a London magazine in 1890, it is an

---

upstart pure and simple, 'without father, without mother, without descent.'

One example that lives on as a classic of this type of note is to be found in Edward Gibbon's monumental work, *The History of the Decline and Fall of the Roman Empire*, of which the best modern edition is that by John Bagnell Bury.

Gibbon is discussing the march of the forces of the First Crusade through the territories of the Byzantine emperor, Alexius I, and the associated reconquest of the ancient city of Nicæa, near Constantinople, from the hands of the Seljuk Sultan Suleiman Kilijarslan I. The Christian army devoted the whole of the period from May 14 to June 20, 1097, to a siege of the city, which finally fell, not to their forces but to the diplomatic efforts of Alexius. The Crusaders, in their zeal, expected to pillage the city, which, after all, was a possession of an Islamic state. Alexius, however, had other ideas. He already was in possession of Suleiman's wife, who had attempted to flee from the besieged town with her retinue, but was intercepted before she could make good her escape. Now he intended both to preserve the city as a valuable economic prize for his state and to improve relations with Suleiman, who might, one day, prove the victor rather than the vanquished, in the fortunes of war which would follow the departure of the Western Christian army towards the east.

Gibbon's note on the word *miscreant* remains as trenchant today as it was in the eighteenth century.

Edward Gibbon, *The History of the Decline and Fall of the Roman Empire*, 7 vols., ed. J. B. Bury (London: Methuen & Co., Ltd., 1912), chapter LVIII, vol. VI, pp. 306–307

In the space of seven weeks much labour and blood were expended, and some progress, especially by Count Raymond, was made on the side of the besiegers. But the Turks could protract their resistance and secure their escape, as long as they were masters of the lake Ascanius, which stretches several miles to the westward of the city. The means of conquest were supplied by the prudence and industry of Alexius; a great number of boats was transported on sledges from the sea to the lake; they were filled with the most dextrous of his archers; the flight of the sultana was intercepted; Nice was invested by land and water; and a Greek emissary persuaded the inhabitants to accept his master's protection, and to save themselves, by a timely surrender, from the rage of the savages of Europe. In the moment of victory, or at least of hope, the crusaders, thirsting for blood and plunder, were awed by the Imperial banner that streamed from the citadel, and Alexius guarded with jealous vigilance this important conquest. The murmurs of the chiefs were stifled by honour or interest; and, after a halt of nine days, they directed their march towards Phrygia, under the guidance of a Greek general, whom they suspected of secret connivance with the sultan. The consort and the principal servants of Soliman had been honourably restored without ransom, and the emperors generosity to the *miscreants*[1] was interpreted as treason to the Christian cause.

[1]. *Mécréant*, a word invented by the French crusaders, and confined in that language to its primitive sense. It should seem that the zeal of our ancestors boiled higher, and that they branded every unbeliever as a rascal. A similar prejudice still lurks in the minds of many who think themselves Christians.

Sometimes, of course, it is not a word but a term or expression, often from the past, that needs a gloss. In the biological sciences this is especially true, because the taxonomy of both living and extinct creatures has undergone several changes, and many elaborations, in this century. Your reader may not know that the particular name of an organism might have been changed several times, even in the past few decades, so that two or more references to the same creature, but under different names, need to be explained carefully in your notes. Much the same thing is true of the names of chemical compounds, mathematical expressions, and other scientific terminology. Only in this way can you maintain the continuity of your discussion without modifying the actual texts of the earlier sources that you quote or to which you refer.

In the following example, drawn from an undergraduate term paper on Thomas Henry Huxley and his perception that there was a close connection between some fossil remnants of dinosaurs and living birds, the author quotes Huxley's proposal to group *Archæopteryx* and some other bird-like reptiles into an order called *Ornithoscelida*, a classification that did not last, and which is unfamiliar to modern readers.

Huxley asserts that *Archaeopteryx* does not represent the only transitional creature between dinosaurs and modern-day birds. Huxley continues his argument by hypothesizing that there was an ancestor of *Archaeopteryx* from which birds also are descended. It is necessary to visualize this earlier connection in order "to understand the manner in which the reptilian has been metamorphosed into the bird type, [which] are really to be found among a group of ancient and extinct terrestrial reptiles known as the *Ornithoscelida*."[1]

---

1. Huxley's term *Ornithoscelida* was for an order in which he proposed to include the *Dinosauria* and *Compsognathus*, because he was not sure whether or not *Compsognathus* was a true dinosaur. I will use the modern term for this group of dinosaurs, *Coelurosauria*, when I am not quoting Huxley directly, but the two terms are, fundamentally, synonymous. For a further discussion of Huxley's views on this classification, see his *Science and Hebrew Tradition*, vol. 4, *Collected Essays* (New York: D. Appleton and Company, 1894; reprint, New York, Greenwood Press, 1968), 103ff. See also Thomas Henry Huxley, "Further Evidence of the Affinity Between the Dinosaurian Reptiles and Birds," *Quarterly Journal of the Geological Society of London* 26 (1870): 12–31; and "On the Animals Which Are Most Nearly Intermediate Between Birds and Reptiles," *Annals and Magazine of Natural History*, 4th ser., no. 2 (February 1868): 62–75.

Of course, this type of footnote is used for much more than the explication of words and phrases. In scientific and mathematical texts, they often are used to describe new uses for old symbols; to define the terms, symbolic and otherwise, that appear in the text more precisely, or to show how the author relates the terms to other works in the field.

A good example of the last case is taken from a recent work in the history of mathematics by an English scholar. His book opens with a long essay on the life and work of the sixteenth-century mathematician, Robert Recorde. As the author states:

> As the writer of the first series of mathematical texts in English, Robert Recorde clearly holds a special place in the history of mathematics education in England. Yet it can be argued that Recorde should be recognised for yet another reason: that he was the first mathematics educator. Not only did Recorde teach mathematics, but his writings show clearly—both implicitly and explicitly—that he had also given serious consideration to the problems of learning and teaching mathematics.[1]

After he reviews the circumstances of Recorde's life and the state of mathematical education in England in his time, the author then considers each of Recorde's own books, one by one, closing with *The Whetstone of Witte*, published in 1557.

---

1. Geoffrey Howson, *A History of Mathematics Education in England* (Cambridge: Cambridge University Press, 1982) 6.

Geoffrey Howson, *A History of Mathematics Education in England*
(Cambridge: Cambridge University Press, 1982) 18–19, 243

'The Whetstone of Witte'

This was the last of Recorde's works to appear
(1557) and the only one never to have been repub-
lished. It was a work dedicated not to a person, but
to a body which sought to promote overseas trade,
the Company of Moscow Adventurers, to which
Recorde acted as adviser. Although generally
thought of as a book on algebra, the *Whetstone* is, in
fact, also much concerned with arithmetic. Described as being 'the seconde parte of Arithmeticke:
containing the [e]xtraction of Rootes: The *Cossike*
practice, with the rule of *Equation*: and the woorkes
of *Surde Nombers*', the book begins with the kind of
arithmetic to be found in Euclid and Boethius in
which the emphasis lies not on commercial applica-
bility but on various kinds of numbers and their
properties.

The algebra contained in the book is based on
German sources and, as Hutton points out in his
Dictionary and his Tracts (vol. 2) in the course of
extensive and still valuable comparative surveys of
books on algebra, Recorde often quotes and takes
examples from Schuebel. Recorde deals with ele-
mentary algebra as far as quadratic equations and
offers some new mathematics, such as techniques
for finding the square roots of algebraic expressions. However, the *Whetstone* is above all remembered for the fact that it was the first English book
to use the + and − notation (following Stifel), and the
first book ever to use the '=' sign to denote equality.
As Recorde put it 'to avoide the tediouse repetition
of these woordes: is equalle to: I will sette as I doe

often in woorke use, a pair of paralleles, or Gemowe [twin, as in gemini] lines of one length, thus =, bicause noe 2 thynges, can be moare equalle.' With the help of this innovation Recorde was able to express equations in a purely symbolic form.[1]

1. The equals symbol was not immediately adopted by mathematicians. Indeed, it was over sixty years before it next appeared in a published book. Then, in 1618, it is to be found in the English translation of Napier's *Descriptio* and later Harriot and Oughtred both adopted it in their influential books. It then rapidly gained more general favour, and alternative uses to denote, for example, arithmetical difference or parallelism declined. That Harriot and Oughtred should use the sign suggests that they were familiar with Recorde's book. It is noteworthy, however, that Wallis in his 1685 *Treatise of Algebra, both Historical and Practical* appears never to have seen the *Whetstone*. He refers merely to the book written 'about the year 1552 (if I be not misinformed)' (p. 63). This, however, may only serve to strengthen the assertion that it was especially the non-university men who were to use and benefit from Recorde's texts.

Of course, it is not only the unusual word or expression that needs this type of footnote. Very often, words which are found in the common vocabulary are taken up with a new or special meaning and become a part of the argot of some profession or intellectual pursuit. Once this has been done, the word itself may undergo several smaller transformations of meaning, embodying subtle distinctions that may be lost easily, if the writer is not careful.

Our next example comes from a small work which explores the newly-discovered universality of phase transitions in such physical diversities as fluids, magnets, and superconductors. After introductory matter which describes the physics that underlie the concept of universality, the author elaborates a series of concepts and definitions which he thinks his readers will need in order to understand the theoretical approaches he will discuss later in the book. The second chapter, "Statistical Mechanics and Thermodynamics," reviews the basic principles of statistical mechanics, thermodynamics, and first-order and continuous phase transitions, among others. Our example is taken from his short section on the last topic.

J. M. Yeomans, *Statistical Mechanics of Phase Transitions*
(Oxford: Clarendon Press, 1992) 21–22

A phase transition is signalled by a singularity in a thermodynamic potential such as the free energy. If there is a finite discontinuity in one or more of the first derivatives of the appropriate thermodynamic potential the transition is termed first-order. For a magnetic system the free energy $\mathscr{F}$, defined by eqn (2.5), is the appropriate potential with discontinuity in the magnetization showing that the transition is first-order. For a fluid the Gibb's free energy, $\mathscr{G} = \mathscr{F} + PV$, is relevant and there are discontinuities in the volume and the entropy across the vapour pressure curve. A jump in the entropy implies that the transition is associated with a latent heat.

If the first derivatives are continuous but second derivatives are discontinuous or infinite the transition will be described as higher order, continuous, or critical.[1] This type of transition corresponds to a divergent susceptibility, an infinite correlation length, and a power law delay of correlations.

1. The term 'second-order' phase transition, used synonymously with continuous phase transition, is a relic of the original classification of phase transitions into first-, second-, third- ... order due to Ehrenfest. This essentially recognized only discontinuities in thermodynamic derivatives, rather than divergences, which has been proved inappropriate. Therefore we follow M. E. Fisher in terming transitions first-order or continuous.

Documenting Contrasting Views

THE FOOTNOTES in which you point your reader to opinions other than your own, or those which are at odds with the prevailing or majority view of some person, event, or idea, are among the most important parts of any paper or book. This is the case because your reader is entitled to know the whole range of legitimate speculation which you have encountered in your own work.

Suppose that you consult twenty sources to gather together as many views as possible about a person or event or thing, for your own learning. Nineteen of those earlier scholars present a view with which you agree, and that is the view you adopt in your paper. Yet, the twentieth, who disagrees entirely with the others, also is a respected scholar with a substantial reputation in the field. Your reader must have the confidence in your work to know that you will not have omitted this twentieth view, even though it conflicts substantially with your own and the views of many others in the field. Of course, you need not search assiduously for comments and opinions by those who are on the "intellectual fringe," but you must not omit the opinions and conclusions of men and women who have reached them only after great study and analysis. You must remember, as you incorporate these notes into your text, that there was a time when Galileo's view of planetary motion was only the opinion of one scholar and was in conflict with the whole accepted view of the universe in his time. Had his ideas not been spread by others who read his work and quoted his views, his intellectual triumph might be lost today. Of course, eventually, the facts he unearthed would have come to light as a product of someone else's work; but there was not need for that, because his own accomplishments were the subject of many discussions in the schools and universities of Europe, in spite of ecclesiastical opposition. That they were discussed, and written about, so extensively is testimony to the willingness of scholars and students, both, to quote and cite opinions that are at variance, often very much at variance, with the accepted "facts" of any time. Much the same can be said about the work of Vesalius or Darwin or Goddard.

Centuries of scholarship rest on the free and open discussion of a wide-ranging collection of views and opinions on nearly every subject, and the reputation of most of the great men and women who have lived the "life of the mind" rests not only on their own discoveries—often quite startling, or even objectionable, to their contemporaries—but also to the vigor and honesty with which their work was discussed by others. The citation, and even extensive discussion, of contrasting views in footnotes is one of the principal ways in which each writer can preserve and protect the atmosphere of intellectual honesty.

We cannot let this opportunity go by without mentioning that works about difficult questions, be they political, philosophical, social, or scientific, which omit notes that discuss conflicting views, or even citations to works where such views can be found, are, in our opinion, intellectually suspect—as is so often the case with books and articles on modern political and social problems in America.

So, do use a footnote to mention, or even to discuss, views that are different from, or even conflict with, your own and those of other scholars whose views you have adopted. In this way, you preserve for your reader the opportunity to learn about varying opinions and intellectual debate, so that he or she can read further on the topic. This kind of note is perhaps the principal example of how footnotes work to preserve intellectual honesty.

Often, in this type of footnote, you will see the abbreviation *cf*, which means *confer*, the Latin equivalent of the English word *compare*. Much of the time, a reference that is introduced with this abbreviation merely points the reader to a text which confirms or elaborates the material that is being discussed. But it also does frequently point the reader to other material which presents a contrasting, or even contradictory, opinion or interpretation—which allows the reader to "compare" the two.

Our first example of this use of the footnote is taken from a modern, general treatise on quantum mechanics. After a lengthy consideration of the structure of quantum theory, the author moves forward to a section in which he discusses the interpretation of quantum theory more specifically. After a consideration of the problem of properties, including experimental questions and the dispersion principle, he begins a review of statistical interpretation, a term which he narrows to be "an interpretation of quantum theory which views the state description provided by the state vector or density operator as applicable to an ensemble of similarly prepared systems, rather than to an individual system." He then restates the principles that he used in defining the method of statistical interpretation in quantum mechanics.

R. I. G. Hughes, *The Structure and Interpretation of Quantum Mechanics* (Cambridge, Massachusetts: Harvard University Press, 1989) 161–162

The view I have sketched here has three components, which can be called the *Precise Value Principle* (PVP), the *Relative Frequency Principle* (RFP), and the *Faithful Measurement Principle* (FMP). . . . According to PVP, whatever the state of a system (or, more properly, of the ensemble containing the system), each observable has a precise value for the individual system. According to RFP, the quantum-mechanical statistics represent the relative frequency of occurrence of these values within the ensemble. FMP suggests that every successful measurement reveals the (preexisting) value of that observable for the particular system under test. FMP thus tells us that, if the value a of an observable A occurs in an ensemble with relative frequency n, then (ideal) measurements of A will yield that value with the same frequency.[1] Thus the measured frequencies coincide with the existing frequencies of particular values, provided, that is, that the measured sample can be thought of as a genuine ensemble.

1. In an acidulous footnote, Fine [Arthur Fine, "How to Count Frequencies, a Primer for Quantum Realists," *Synthese*, 42:145–154] disputes this correlation, but his rejection to it seems, instead, to be a rejection of FMP.

One use for this type of footnote that can be especially valuable is a discussion of some point of reasoning or explanation which is different from the one you have adopted in your paper, yet one which reaches the same conclusion—getting to the station by a different route. By offering your reader other rational pathways to the same conclusion, you enhance greatly the probability that your own reasoning will be understood. Indeed, however correct your principles of reasoning may be, the trail of your explanation may be as impenetrable to one reader as it is transparent and perfectly orderly to another. If you can show another method by which the same conclusion, or at least the same progress of reasoning, can be attained, your reader may well grasp the point you wish to make more readily, and will thank you for it heartily.

The following example is taken from David Hackett Fischer's important and valuable treatise, *Historians' Fallacies*. In his chapter on the fallacies of factual significance, he addresses the question of the non-existence of the "whole truth."

David Hackett Fischer, *Historian's Fallacies: Toward a Logic of Historical Thought* (New York: Harper & Row, Publishers, 1970) 66

A historian who swears to tell nothing but the whole truth, would thereby take a vow of eternal silence. A researcher who promises to find the whole secret for himself condemns himself to perpetual failure. The whole truth, at any stage of an inquiry, is an ideal that ought to be abolished from historiography, for it cannot ever be attained. Historians are bound to tell the best and biggest truths they can discover, but these truths are very different from the whole truth, which does not and cannot exist. A scholar who seeks the whole truth is on a road which can only end in the intellectual side of relativism, or else in that condition of methodological anomie which characterizes so many of my colleagues.

Georg Wilhelm Friedrich Hegel, poor twisted Teutonic soul that he was, is an easy mark for a methodologist. Most of the fallacies in this book could be illustrated by his arguments. But there are many other examples of the holist fallacy, which is an exceedingly common form of error. All metahistorians, by definition, are guilty of this mistake— Toynbee, Spengler, Sorokin, Marx, Comte, Kant, Condorcet, Vico—and others who have tried to discover the "meaning" of *the* whole past.[1]

1. Arthur Danto reaches the same conclusion by a different argument. He argues that the significance of events is always, in part, dependent on later events; and therefore, that the significance of past events is partly dependent on future events; and thus, that substantive philosophers of history are condemned to failure in their quest for the whole truth, for their method would require a "history of events before the events themselves have happened" [Arthur Coleman Danto, *Analytical Phi-*

losophy of History (Cambridge: Cambridge University Press, 1965) 14]. This is not to say that the past can change, for events happened in the way that they happened, and not in any other way. But facts, or true statements about past events, can and will change, as other events occur.

One special variety of this type of note is used to correct the errors in published materials that you found in your own research—and you will find many of them, because all of us are fallible, even the most renowned scholars. You can use this footnote to document facts which have become garbled, such as discrepancies in dates of birth or death which appear in your sources. Sometimes, you will find errors of larger importance, such as the misattribution of a published work to the wrong author or errors in detailing the family background or ancestry of a person. Such mistakes, by the way, often are repeated, again and again, through a genealogy of errors. This happens when a writer misquotes or misnotes factual matters from a primary source, and, later, other writers copy the original errors by relying on the scholarship of the first researcher, without checking the primary sources themselves. The effect of this shoddy method by later writers is to proliferate the error from one article or book to many articles and many books.

Perhaps the most famous example of this stream of errors is the often-repeated assertion that it was Christopher Columbus who first had the idea that the world was a globe, and then set out to prove it. In fact, the spherical nature of the world was well understood, probably from prehistoric times. Every person who moved upon a sea, or even upon a large lake, out of the sight of land will have noticed, on her return if not upon her departure, that the landforms appear to roll up upon the horizon as if both they and the viewer were on the surface of a sphere. Aristotle offered an observational proof of the Earth's sphericity by noting that the curved shadow which appears to travel across the face of the moon during a lunar eclipse is, in fact, the limb of the Earth itself. And Eratosthenes, a little more than a century later, used the fundamentals of plane trigonometry to measure the circumference of the globe to a very high degree of accuracy. The difficulties in understanding came later, with the work of the Egypto-Roman astronomer, Claudius Ptolemæus, who argued that Eratosthenes's figure of about twenty-four thousand modern miles was too great by a large margin. Thereafter, Europeans debated the relative merits of Eratosthenes's discoveries and Ptolemy's refutations for

centuries, finally concluding that the earlier Greek was right
and the later Roman was wrong. Columbus espoused the views
of Ptolemy and, since the land distance from western Europe
to the Asian Pacific region was known with some accuracy, he
concluded that he needed to sail but a short distance to the
west to come upon the islands of Japan. Of course, it was Eratosthenes who was right, after all, and had Columbus not
strayed upon the New World when he was perilously close to
the end of his supply of food and water, he would have faced
the Pacific Ocean and certain death. Columbus also erred in
not understanding the logistical limits of the ships he had at his
disposal. Crossing from Spain to Japan by traveling westward
presents no difficulty for the *Queen Elizabeth II*, but in a ship
of the size of the *Santa Maria* there was no room to carry the
necessary food, water, and other supplies for such a voyage.

A considerable body of serious scholarship has been devoted
to an effort to discover who first stated that it was, indeed,
Columbus who thought the world was round, but no satisfac-
tory answer has ever been forthcoming. What remains is the
fact that this error has been perpetuated by copying from one
source to another, and from the voice of teachers to the ears of
pupils, for more than a century. It will not die.

Of course, when you correct the errors of others, do so with
kindness, in the hope that later writers will be as kind when
they correct yours.

Our example of this type of note is taken from a wide-ranging consideration of the uses of mythology in the literature of
the English Renaissance by one of Harvard University's most
distinguished teacher-scholars. Douglas Bush was not particularly kind in his corrective notes, which is, perhaps, the only
fault we can find with this example.

Early in his book, Bush has reached the point at which he
discusses William Painter's significant contribution to Elizabethan literature, *The Palace of Pleasure*, which contains many
stories derived from the writings of Classical authors. Bush
notes that many earlier writers on, and editors of, Painter had
drawn up lists that showed Painter's sources, but had made
many mistakes in their attributions.

Douglas Bush, *Mythology and the Renaissance Tradition in English Poetry*, rew rev. ed. (New York: W. W. Norton & Company, Inc. 1963), 33–34

III. CLASSICAL TALES IN ENGLISH PROSE

Painter's *Palace of Pleasure* (1566–1567), which introduced Italian and French novelle to English readers and especially to English dramatists, concerns us here on account of its forty-one classical stories. The sources make a significant list: Herodotus (two stories); Aelian (three); Plutarch's *Morals* (one); Aulus Gellius (twelve); Livy (eight); Quintus Curtius (three); Xenophon (one); Pedro Mexia (two); Guevara's *Letters* (three); Bandello (six).¹ The collection was indeed put together to be "delectable . . . for al sortes of men."

1. The correct list of sources is taken from my article on Painter, "The Classical Tales in Painter's Palace of Pleasure," *Journal of English and Germanic Philology*, vol. XXIII, no. 3 (July 1924), 331ff. The list in Jacobs' edition [William Painter, *The Palace of Pleasure: Elizabethan Versions of Italian and French Novels from Boccaccio, Bandello, Cinthio, Straparola, Queen Margaret of Navarre, and Others*, 3 vols., Joseph Jacobs, ed. (London: D. Nutt, 1890)], which is repeated in the *Dictionary of National Biography*, is full of errors, including such an absurdity as making Tacitus the source of the account of Queen Zenobia. These errors are repeated again in Peter Haworth's volume of selections from Painter, *An Elizabethan Story-Book[: Famous Tales from the Palace of Pleasure* (London and New York: Longmans, Green, and Co., Ltd., 1928)]; when he touches on sources, in E. A. Baker's *History of the English Novel*, II {E[rnest] A[lbert] Baker, *History of the English Novel*, vol. 2, *The Elizabethan Age and After* (London: H. F. & G. Witherby, 1929)}; and in the edition of Painter issued in 1929 by the Cresset Press [William Painter, *The Palace of Pleasure*, 4 vols., Hamish Miles, ed. (London: Cresset Press, 1929)].

From Livy Painter took the stories of the Horatii and the Curiatii, Lucrece, Mucius Scaevola, Coriolanus, Appius and Virginia, Camillus, Tanaquil, and Thoxena; from Herodotus (Valla's translation apparently) the stories of Candaules and Gyges, Solon and Croesus; from Xenophon the story of Panthea; from Plutarch that of Timoclea; from Bandello, Antiochus, Ariobarzanes, Aristotimus, Sophonisba, Pompey and the lady of Hidrusa, Faustina; from [Bishop Antonio de]Guevara the correspondence of Trajan and Plutarch, the lives of the courtesans Lamia, Lais, and Flora (as examples to be avoided), and the energetic Queen Zenobia; from a French version of Mexia, the accounts of Timon and the Amazons; and so forth.

Greek authors were translated from Latin versions. In rendering Xenophon, Painter even made wholesale use of William Barkar's English translation of six books of the *Cyropaedia* [*The VIII. Bookes of Xenophon, containinge the Institutiõ, schole, and education of Cyrus, the noble Kinge of Persye: also his ciuill and princelye estate, his expedition into Babylon, Syria and Aegypt, and his exhortation before his death, to his children.* Translated out of Greeke into Englishe by M. William Bercker. Imprinted Anno Domini MDLXVII]. He likewise took some liberal extracts from Brende's version of Quintus Curtius [*The historie of Qvintvs Curcius, conteyning the actes of the Greate Alexander,* translated out of Latine into Englishe by John Brende. 1553. Imprinted at London by Rycharde Tottell].

Our next example requires some explanation, because we take you suddenly into the midst of one of the most distinguished critical considerations of the work of the American novelist, Stephen Crane. In chapter six of his book, Milne Holton begins his discussion of Crane's masterpeice, *The Red Badge of Courage*. He leads his reader towards an understanding of one of the central moments in the novella; that point, at the end of chapter nine, in which Henry Fleming, the hero of the work, experiences the death of his friend, Jim:

> His tall figure stretched itself to its full height. There was a slight rending sound. Then it began to swing forward, slow and straight, in the manner of a falling tree. A swift muscular contortion made the left shoulder strike the ground first.
>
> The body seemed to bounce a little way from the earth. "God!" said the tattered soldier.
>
> The youth had watched, spellbound, this ceremony at the place of meeting. His face had been twisted into an expression of every agony he had imagined for his friend.
>
> He now sprang to his feet and, going closer, gazed upon the pastelike face. The mouth was open and the teeth showed in a laugh.
>
> As the flap of the blue jacket fell away from the body, he could see that the side looked as if it had been chewed by wolves.
>
> The youth turned, with sudden, livid rage, toward the battlefield. He shook his fist. He seemed about to deliver a philippic.
>
> "Hell—"
>
> The red sun was pasted in the sky like a wafer.[1]

With this text in mind, the last words of the chapter, we now can appreciate Holton's systematic review, in a well-placed footnote, of the various, and very contradictory, critical opinions about the significance of the last sentence, with its famous simile, "The red sun was pasted in the sky like a wafer."

---

1. Stephen Crane, *The Red Badge of Courage* (New York: Dover Publications, Inc., 1990) 43.

Milne Holton, *Cylinder of Vision: The Fiction and Journalistic Writing of Stephen Crane* (Baton Rouge: Louisiana State University Press, 1972) 103

"The youth, aghast and filled with wonder at the tall soldier, began quaveringly to question him. 'Where yeh goin', Jim? What you thinking about? Where you going? Tell me, won't you, Jim?' The tall soldier faced about as upon relentless pursuers. In his eyes there was a great appeal. 'Leave me be, can't yeh? Leave me be fer a minnit.'"[1] Henry can only stand by, helpless and apart, and watch in horror the grotesque rite of his friend's death. And— with phrases like "the tremor of his legs caused him to bounce a little way from the earth" or "the teeth showed in a laugh" or "the side looked as if it had been chewed by wolves"—the rendering is grotesque indeed. Here again, as in the earlier works, the grotesque rendering records the distortion of the protagonist's emotions. For now Henry is at a moment of intense isolation and intense awareness. His only relief is in gesture. It is here that Henry curses the sun, the implacable and distant center of his universe.[2]

1. Stephen Crane, *The Red Badge of Courage: An Episode of the American Civil War*, in Thomas A. Gullason, ed., *The Complete Novels of Stephen Crane* (Garden City, New York: Doubleday and Company, 1967) 242.
2. I shall confine further comment on the now stale wafer of Crane's final sentence in Chap. 9 to this footnote. First, I would suggest again that the significance lies, not in the objective meaning of the symbol, but in its significance as the object of the boy's anger. The field is indeed an embattled one, occupied by such figures as Joseph Hergesheimer [in Wilson Follett, ed., *The Work of Stephen Crane*, 12 vols. (New York: Alfred A. Knopf, 1925–1927), vol. I, p. x]; R[obert] W[ooster] Stallman, ed., *Stephen Crane: An Omnibus* (New York: Alfred A. Knopf, 1952) 199–200; and his "The Scholar's Net" [in *College English*

XVII (October, 1955)] 20-27; his "Fiction and Its Critics," in his *The Houses that James Built and Other Literary Studies* (East Lansing, Michigan: Michigan State University Press, 1961) 247–248; Philip Rahv, "Fiction and the Criticism of Fiction," [in *Kenyon Review* XVIII (Spring, 1956)] 276–299; Scott C. Osborn, "Stephen Crane's Imagery: 'Pasted Like a Wafer'" [in *American Literature* XXIII (November, 1951)] 362; James B. Colvert, "The Origins of Stephen Crane's Literary Creed," [in *University of Texas Studies in English* XXXIV (1955)] 183; Eric W. Colson, "Crane's *The Red Badge of Courage*, IX," [in *Explicator* XVI (March, 1958)], Item 34; and Cecil D. Eby, Jr., who denies any symbolic intent whatsoever, in "Stephen Crane's 'Fierce Red Wafer,'" [in *English Language Notes* I (December, 1963)] 128–130. But in Stallman's biography [*Stephen Crane: A Biography* (New York: George Brazillier, 1968)] 171–176, Stallman's position is again asserted and developed further.

A still, small voice in *College English*, who suggests that the wafer which Crane had in mind was that red seal affixed to a document and implying finality, seems—in spite of Professor Stallman's somewhat illogical objection—to be closest to the truth. See Rudolph Von Abele in "Symbolism and the Student," *College English* XVI (April, 1955) 427.

Crane's wafer simile, by the way, in its fresh and diminishing effect, is in no way atypical of Crane's style (the boat as bathtub in "The Open Boat" will be another example). But regardless of the simile, the sun—occurring as it does here and elsewhere in the novel—is again symbolically significant.

Asides and Commentaries

THE ASIDE or commentary is the place where the author can address her reader personally on some point which she would like to add, but which is really an addendum to the discussion or entirely divorced from it. Using this kind of note allows the author to make direct, conversational connections to the reader without disrupting the flow of the essay.

In such a note, it is common to change the tone of the discourse, which can be an opportunity for the author to add whimsicality or amusement to material which might otherwise be dry.

This type of note also allows the author to add facts or commentary which she thinks the reader might like to know, just for the sake of intellectual curiosity.

While creating this note may be tricky, and can be overdone, it is, at its best, one that will bring a decided reaction from the reader, from a smile to an audible expression of discovery.

Our first example comes from the vademecum[1] of every graduate student in English literature, Richard D. Altick's *The Art of Literary Research*. Here is a portion of his discussion on the appropriate use of footnotes in a scholarly paper.

1. *Vademecum*, from the Latin *vade*, the singular imperative of *vadere* ("to go") and *me-cum* ("with me"). A manual of ready reference that is often carried about by the reader. For an elaboration of this definition together with illustrative quotations, see *The Oxford English Dictionary*, 2nd ed., 20 vols. (Oxford Clarendon Press, 1989), s. v. "vade-mecum."

Richard D. Altick, *The Art of Literary Research*, rev. ed. (New York: W. W. Norton & Company, Inc., 1975) 219 and n. 20

Now a word about documentation. A superstition akin to the one about avoiding the first person singular holds that the scholarly quality of a paper is directly proportional to the number of footnotes, as if the heavy ballast at the bottom of each page insures against the balloon's soaring errantly into Cloud-Cuckoo-Land. No such thing. Footnotes, it is said, are for use, not ostentation.[1] They have two purposes. "Documentary" footnotes provide the reader with the sources of all the facts, as well as the opinions that are not original with the writer, so that if he is at all skeptical, he can check for himself. Moreover, they are an indispensable courtesy to later scholars who may wish to utilize some of the material and need clear directions as to where to find it. "Substantive" footnotes allow the writer a place to put incidental but relevant comment which would interrupt the flow of discourse in the text proper.

1. *Cf.* the Roman emperor in Gibbon's *Decline and Fall of the Roman Empire* (Chapter 7): "Twenty-two acknowledged concubines, and a library of sixty-two thousand volumes, attested the variety of his inclinations; and from the productions which he left behind him, it appears that the former as well as the latter were designed for use rather than ostentation."

One of the great benefits of having the footnote available as a place to make an aside is that you can inject a note of humor into a discussion which may, by necessity, be somewhat dense or complex. Your direct speech to the reader may well be on a topic which is related only tangentially to the subject of your paper, but it can reinforce an important point which you wish your reader both to understand and to remember.

The following example is taken from a once well known text on the methods and techniques that are used to do research on English literary topics. The subject of the discourse is the principles involved in editing literary texts professionally. After setting forth the basic tenets in detail, the author continues by giving some specific examples of these principles at work. In our excerpt, we include three of his notes. Notice how the second one acts to relieve the large body of information that is conveyed in the other two.

Throughout his book, Sanders uses a number of conventional abbreviations frequently. Two of them appear in these notes, *PMLA* for the *Publications of the Modern Language Association of America,* and *MP* for the journal *Modern Philology.*

Chauncey Sanders, *An Introduction to Research in English Literary History* (New York: The Macmillan Company, 1952) 110–111

To discover the *filiation*, or relationship, of a considerable number of texts—as in the manuscripts of Chaucer's *Canterbury Tales*, for example—is sometimes a matter so difficult and so complex as to be beyond the province of this book.[1] One suggestion as to method that may appropriately be made here, however, is that no reliance is to be placed upon the agreement of two texts in a correct reading as an indication that one of them is derived from the other; an editor, a compositor, a proofreader—where manuscripts are involved, a scribe—may easily hit upon a right reading in attempting to correct a mistake, and may do so quite independently of any text containing the proper reading. Only when two texts have errors in common—and a convincing number of such errors[2]—

1. The *Canterbury Tales* problem is discussed at length in *The Text of the Canterbury Tales, studied on the basis of all known manuscripts,* 8 vols., ed. John Matthews Manly and Margaret Josephine Rickert (Chicago: University of Chicago Press, 1940), Vol. II; see also Germaine Dempster, "Manly's Conception of the Early History of the *Canterbury Tales*," *PMLA*, LXI (1946): 379–415. Anyone interested in such problems should read: W. W. Greg, *The Calculus of Variants: An Essay on Textual Criticism* (Oxford: Clarendon Press, 1927); William P. Shepard, "Recent Theories of Textual Criticism," *MP*, XXVIII (1931): 129–141; and W. W. Greg, "Recent Theories of Textual Criticism," *MP*, XXVIII (1931): 401–404.

2. When I found two examination papers both containing the rather startling information that Thomas à Becket was a young monk of the seventeenth century whom the pilgrims in Chaucer's *Canterbury Tales* were on their way to Canterbury to kill, I had very little doubt that one of those papers was derived from the other.

can one say with assurance that there is a textual relationship.[3]

3. Even then one cannot say that A is copied from B or B from A; both may be derived from an earlier text X, or Y may have been derived from A and B from Y, or A may have been derived from X and B from Z, which latter was derived from either A or X. And of course other combinations are possible. Dr. McKerrow suggested [Ronald McKerrow, *Prolegomena for the Oxford Shakespeare: A Study in Editorial Method* (Oxford: Clarendon Press, 1939) 13]: "It would, I think, be convenient if we could use some such word as 'monogenous' and 'polygenous' to designate the two groupings of texts . . . : 'monogenous' standing for those which derive from a single extant edition and 'polygenous' for those which have at their head two or more extant editions none of which derives from another—substantive texts, as I have called them. . . ."

Walt Whitman wrote one of the most interesting American literary footnotes at the very beginning of his prose collection, *Specimen Days & Collect*. For many years, Whitman kept an extensive series of notebooks and jottings from which, in his old age, he made selections and then collated them into a single volume. From the opening page of the book, Whitman wishes his readers to know something of the antecedents of the work in these earlier writings, so he inserted a digressive, but informative, note to tell his readers about how he came to write the notebooks and then to create the collection from them upon which his readers are about to embark.

Walt Whitman, *Specimen Days & Collect* (Philadelphia: Rees Welsh, 1882) 1–2

SPECIMEN DAYS
A HAPPY HOUR'S COMMAND

Down in the Woods, July 2d, 1882—If I do it at all I must delay no longer. Incongruous and full of skips and jumps as is that huddle of diary-jottings, war memoranda of 1862–'65, Nature notes of 1877–'81, with Western and Canadian observations afterward, all bundled up and tied by a big string, the resolution and indeed mandate comes to me this day, this hour (and what a day! what an hour just passing! the luxury of riant grass and blowing breeze, with all the shows of sun and sky and perfect temperature, never before so filling me body and soul)—to go home, untie the bundle, reel out diary scraps and memoranda, just as they are, large or small, one after another, into print pages,[1] and let the mélange's lackings and wants of connection take care of themselves.

1. The pages from 18 to 34 are nearly verbatim an offhand letter of mine in January, 1882, to an insisting friend. Following, I give some gloomy experiences. The war of attempted secession has, of course, been the distinguishing event of my time. I commenced at the close of 1862, and continued steadily through '63, '64, and '65, to visit the sick and wounded of the army, both on the field and in the hospitals in and around Washington city. From the first I kept little notebooks for impromptu jottings in pencil to refresh my memory of names and circumstances, and what was specially wanted, etc. In these I briefed cases, persons, sights, occurrences in camp, by the bedside, and not seldom by the corpses of the dead. Some were scratched down from narratives I heard and itemized while watching, or waiting, or tending somebody amid those scenes. I have dozens of such little notebooks left, never to be possibly said or sung. I wish I could convey to the reader the associa-

tions that attach to these soiled and creased livraisons, each composed of a sheet or two of paper, folded small to carry in the pocket, and fastened with a pin. I leave them just as I threw them by after the war, blotched here and there with more than one bloodstain, hurriedly written, sometimes at the clinic, not seldom amid the excitement of uncertainty, or defeat, or of action, or getting ready for it, or a march. Most of the pages from 42 to 113 are verbatim copies of those lurid and blood-smutched little notebooks.

Very different are most of the memoranda that follow. Some time after the war ended I had a paralytic stroke, which prostrated me for several years. In 1876 I began to get over the worst of it. From this date, portions of several seasons, especially summers, I spent at a secluded haunt down in Camden County, New Jersey—Timber Creek, quite a little river (it enters from the great Delaware, twelve miles away)— with primitive solitudes, winding stream, recluse and woody banks, sweet-feeding springs, and all the charms that birds, grass, wild-flowers, rabbits and squirrels, old oaks, walnut trees, etc., can bring. Through these times, and on these spots, the diary from page 115 onward was mostly written.

(The COLLECT afterward gathers up the odds and ends of whatever pieces I can now lay hands on, written at various times past, and swoops all together like fish in a net.)

I suppose I publish and leave the whole gathering, first, from that eternal tendency to perpetuate and preserve what is behind all Nature, authors included; second, to symbolize two or three specimen interiors, personal and other, out of the myriads of my time, the middle range of the nineteenth century in the New World: a strange, unloosened, wondrous time. But the book is probably without any definite purpose that can be told in a statement.

Throughout this section of our book, we have mentioned the quality of humor several times; and, indeed, there have been notes whose sole purpose was to bring a smile to the reader. We cannot end this section without an example of the classical American humorous footnote from that master of the genre, Will Cuppy.[2] His best-known book, *The Decline and Fall of Practically Everybody*, was left as an incomplete manuscript when he died and was edited and published by his friend, Fred Feldkamp. In a series of small vignettes, accompanied by footnotes, Cuppy presents "everything you ever need to know about" many of the major figures of the past.

Our excerpt is taken from his chapter on Henry VIII of England at the point where he is enumerating Henry's litany of wives.

2. Because Will Cuppy seems to be in danger of being forgotten by modern readers, it may be worthwhile to give a few details of his life and works. Cuppy was born William Jacob Cuppy in Auburn, Indiana, on August 23, 1884. He went on to the University of Chicago, from which he earned the degree of bachelor of philosophy in 1907. Three years later, he published his first book, *Maroon Tales: University of Chicago Stories*. Later, he served as an officer in World War I. For many years, Cuppy was a part of the editorial staff of the New York *Herald Tribune*. His books include *How to be a Hermit, or A Bachelor Keeps House* (1929), *How to Tell Your Friends from the Apes* (1931)—the first of a series of books on animals, birds, and fish, that included *How to Become Extinct* (1941) and *How to Attract the Wombat* (1949)—and the posthumously-published *The Decline and Fall of Practically Everybody*. Cuppy also provided the footnotes to *Garden Rubbish and Other Country Bumps* by Walter Carruthers Sellar and Robert Julian Yeatman (London: Methuen, 1936). Cuppy died in New York on September 19, 1949. For a brief notice of him, see Clarence L. Barnhart, ed., *The New Century Cyclopedia of Names*, 3 vols. (New York: Appleton-Century-Crofts, Inc., 1954) I:1151. The world needs a good biography of Will Cuppy.

Will Cuppy, *The Decline and Fall of Practically Everybody*, ed.
Fred Feldkamp (New York: Henry Holt and Company, 1950)
167–169

Catherine of Aragon was one of the most virtuous women who ever lived and she didn't mind saying so. Henry often told her to get the hell out, but she couldn't understand English. She seldom smiled.[1] Later on, she became contumacious and was declared null and void *ab initio*. She had been sort of wished on him, anyway.[2]

Anne Boleyn was younger and prettier and she was not aloof.[3] She was very witty and quick at repartée. That sort of thing is all right for a while, but it seldom pays in the long run. Strangely enough, she wore black satin nightgowns lined with black taffeta and stiffened with buckram.[4] She gave birth to Queen Elizabeth in 1533 and was beheaded by an elegant, two-handed broadsword.

Professor Pollard says of Anne: "Her place in English history is due solely to the circumstances that she appealed to the less refined part of Henry's nature." There you have it.[5]

The rest of Henry's wives were run-of-the-mill.

1. Why should she? The joke was on her.
2. Catherine of Aragon was largely responsible for the revival of horticulture in England.
3. He married her because she was different. But she was too different.
4. Chamberlin states that at night nearly all retired nude, except the very highest, who had only then begun to wear any night clothing at all. Henry's habits in this respect can easily be imagined.
5. In London, not so long ago, the County Council rejected the suggestion that a new street be named after Anne Boleyn. Dr. Emil Davies said that young ladies of today might be stimulated to ask who she was, and "who knows what consequences might ensue?"

Jane Seymour had Edward VI and died of excitement. Anne of Cleves had been much admired in the Low Countries, but in England she just wouldn't do. The way she got herself up, they thought she was playing charades.[6] Anne of Cleves couldn't play or sing like Anne Boleyn. She could only spin, and nobody asked her to spin. Henry had seen her portrait by Holbein. She was a picture bride.[7] Cromwell, who had helped arrange the wedding, was beheaded nineteen days after the divorce.[8] After the divorce, she became twice as beautiful as before, but she was still very plain. She never married again. She'd had enough.

Catherine Howard was beheaded for committing high treason with Francis Dereham and Thomas Culpepper.[9] When Henry heard of her treason, he burst into tears. I guess he was pretty discouraged.

Henry didn't give them much warning. It was all over before they knew it.

Catherine Parr didn't matter. She never committed even low treason.[10]

6. She may have been.
7. It didn't look much like her, actually.
8. Henry should have beheaded Holbein instead.
9. Henry gave her twenty-three quilts before they were married. Subtle, wasn't he?
10. She must have been pretty smart. She outlived him.

We chose our final example to illustrate the use of a commentary to elucidate evidence. The whole documentation which supports some new, or radical, or rediscovered conclusion may well be too unwieldy to incorporate into your text, even though the evidence you have found may be vital to it.

Recently, a respected scholar in Victorian literature and culture used a footnote to provide his readers with all of the surviving physical evidence about a point in the life and intellectual development of William Morris, the artist, craftsman, and firebrand.

Writers about Morris for many years have repeated the assertion that he first became interested in medieval art when he visited the Bodleian Library while he was an undergraduate in Exeter College at the University of Oxford. There, he is said to have seen the wonderful illuminated manuscripts that are so important a part of its collection. On the surface, such a contention appears to be very plausible, indeed. But, in Morris's time, undergraduates were not permitted to view the medieval manuscipts in the Bodleian—a regulation which escaped the attention of earlier researchers—so it is nearly impossible that Moris's first interest in medieval art came from this exposure. In considering Morris's university career, William S. Peterson examined the records of the Bodleian to determine just when Morris did see these famous illuminations. In a carefully-crafted footnote in the second chapter of his work, *The Kelmscott Press*, he marshalls all of the documentation which shows just when Morris visited the Bodleian, which corrects a long-standing error in interpreting Morris's artistic interests and presents clearly the primary evidence for this correction. Note that his use of the footnote as a site for this evidence allows him to present all of the relevant information without breaking the flow of his narrative.

William S. Peterson, *The Kelmscott Press: A History of William Morris's Typographical Adventure* (Oxford: Clarendon Press, 1991) 45, 337–338

In the last year of his life Morris told Wilfrid Scawen Blunt, 'I remember as a boy going into Canterbury Cathedral and thinking that the gates of heaven had been opened to me. Also when I first saw an illuminated manuscript, these first pleasures which I discovered for myself were stronger than anything else in life.' (This close identification of the Gothic cathedral and the Gothic book in Morris's mind is significant: in the 1890s he was to speak of the arrangement of the Kelmscott Press *Chaucer* as purely architectural.) In the Bodleian Library at Oxford, Morris had his first opportunity to examine a large number of illuminated manuscripts, and he was to recall frequently in later years the pleasure he found in them, especially the 'Douce Apocalypse' and a fifteenth-century 'Romance of Alexander'.[1]

1. F. S. Ellis, 'The Life-Work of William Morris', *Journal of the Society of Arts*, 46 (27 May 1898), 620. It is difficult to determine precisely what manuscripts Morris saw in the Bodleian. As an undergraduate he would not have been allowed to use the Bodleian under normal circumstances, and his name does not appear in the library's records during those years. Yet Morris had vivid memories of studying the Bodleian manuscripts, and possibly he might have used the reading room by special permission, and the documents might have been requested by a companion. Morris's name does figure in the Bodleian's 'L.P. Lending Book' after he received his degree, but here the evidence is complicated by the occasional appearance of an 'R. Morris' (probably the Revd Richard Morris, Winchester Lecturer on English Language and Literature at King's College School, London) in the records. 'Mr Morris' (not always, therefore, demonstrably William Morris) called for the following manuscripts (identified by Bodleian shelfmarks): (1) Bod. 264 – 27 Apr. 1856 (certainly William Morris, because 'of Exeter' is

added after the name); (2) Auct. F. IV. 32 – 26 Sept. 1856; (3) Ashmole 789, 1114 – 2 Jan. 1863; (4) Dugdale A1. – 4 May 1865; (5) Auct. F. 38 18 Nov. 1865; (6) Auct. Q – 25 Nov. 1865; (7) Fairfax 14; Ashmole 43, 50, 53, 781 – 2 Jan. 1866; (8) Auct. L. IV. 30 – 1 June 1866; (9) Auct. π. R. IV. 2, 3 – 9 Nov. 1866; (10) Auct. π. Q. inf. π. 5 – 9 Mar. 1867; (11) Douce 381, 302 – 17 May 1867. In a later 'L.P. Entry Book' it is recorded that Morris (accompanied by Emery Walker) came on 28 Nov. 1894 to inspect the 'Douce Apocalypse' (Douce 180) and several other manuscripts: Auct. D. 4. 17; Douce 366; Bod. 264. On this occasion Morris was investigating the possibility of publishing a facsimile of the Apocalypse: see *Bibliography*, p. 151.

Footnoting Relationships & Associations

You **SHOULD** use a footnote to identify and make clear the relationships between or among people, especially—but also between persons and things that are associated with them.

Consider how much more interesting the following passage from Jane Austen's novel, *Emma*, is because of one explanatory note. By the time the reader reaches chapter eight of the novel, she begins to learn of the love of Frank Churchill, recently made very rich by the death of his aunt, for the young, talented, but poor, Jane Fairfax. At a dinner party that is attended by nearly all of the principal characters in the novel, including Frank and Jane, the conversation turns to the anonymous gift of a Broadwood piano, sent to Jane Fairfax, to her considerable amazement:

> The party was rather large, as it included one other family, a proper unobjectionable country family, whom the Coles had the advantage of naming among their acquaintance, and the male part of Mr. Cox's family, the lawyer of Highbury. The less worthy females were to come in the evening, with Miss Bates, Miss Fairfax, and Miss Smith; but already, at dinner, they were too numerous for any subject of conversation to be general; and, while politics and Mr. Elton were talked over, Emma could fairly surrender all her attention to the pleasantness of her neighbour. The first remote sound to which she felt herself obliged to attend, was the name of Jane Fairfax. Mrs. Cole seemed to be relating something of her that was expected to be very interesting. She listened, and found it well worth listening to. That very dear part of Emma, her fancy, received an amusing supply. Mrs. Cole was telling that she had been calling on Miss Bates, and as soon as she entered the room had been struck by the sight of a pianoforte—a very elegant looking instrument—not a grand, but a large-sized square pianoforte; and the substance of the story, the end of all the dialogue which ensued of surprize, and inquiry, and congratulations on her side, and explanations on Miss Bates's, was, that this pianoforte had arrived from Broadwood's[1] the day before, to the great aston-

1. John Broadwood (Cockburnspath, Scotland, 1732–London, 1812) began

ishment of both aunt and niece—entirely unexpected; that at
first, by Miss Bates's account, Jane herself was quite at a loss,
quite bewildered to think who could possibly have ordered it—
but now, they were both perfectly satisfied that it could be from
only one quarter;—of course it must be from Colonel Campbell.

"One can suppose nothing else," added Mrs. Cole, "and I was
only surprized that there could ever have been a doubt. But
Jane, it seems, had a letter from them very lately, and not a word
was said about it. She knows their ways best; but I should not
consider their silence as any reason for their not meaning to
make the present. They might chuse to surprize her."[2]

Footnotes which describe relationships, such as this one
about the Broadwood piano, offer your reader the chance to
understand the material in the text more completely. This particular note offers the modern reader of Austen's novel a greater
understanding of image and nuance which might otherwise
pass unnoticed, thus opening more fully Jane Austen's work,
and her world.

A further example of how a footnote can illuminate a relationship and, thereby, lead to greater understanding is shown

---

his career as a cabinet maker. He joined the harpsichord maker, Burkat Shudi
(Burkhard Tschudi), as an assistant in 1761; and, in 1769, married Barbara,
Shudi's daughter. In the following year, he became a partner in the firm. In
1773, he introduced a new design for a square piano for which he obtained a
patent. Further improvements made his instruments superior to those of any
other maker, as Franz Joseph Haydn noted when he visited Broadwood's shop
in 1794. By then, John Broadwood was the foremost piano maker in Europe.
His instruments were owned and prized by the principal composers and per-
formers of Europe from the end of the eighteenth century until well into the
twentieth. For further information, see Stanley Sadie, ed., *The New Grove
Dictionary of Music and Musicians*, 20 vols. (London: Macmillan Publishers
Limited, 1980) 3:324–325. For a relation of how Thomas Broadwood, son of
John, presented one of the firm's pianos to Beethoven, see Alexander Whee-
lock Thayer, *Thayer's Life of Beethoven*, rev. and ed. by Elliot Forbes, 2 vols.
(Princeton, New Jersey: Princeton University Press, 1964) II:694–696.

Frank Churchill's anonymous gift to Jane Fairfax was truly spectacular, as
Jane Austen knew that her contemporary readers would understand.

2. Jane Austen, *Emma*, The Project Gutenberg Etext, Etext 158, August,
1994 (URL: ftp://mrcnext.cso.uiuc.edu:/pub/etext/etext94/emma10.txt),
chapter VIII, para. 13.

in this annotated letter from George Allan Cate's edition of *The Correspondence of Thomas Carlyle and John Ruskin*. Cate explains carefully why he believes that the "good . . . young English Merchant" is William George Richardson, and goes on to cite two other sources which corroborate his surmises, an unpublished letter from Ruskin to J. R. Severn, now in the manuscript collection of the Bembridge School, Isle of Wight, and a passage in volume two of the published edition of Ruskin's diaries.[3]

3. Joan Evans and John Howard Whitehouse, eds., *The Diaries of John Ruskin*, 3 vols. (Oxford: Clarendon Press, 1956–1959), vol. II, *1848–1873*, 692.

George Allan Cate, ed., *The Correspondence of Thomas Carlyle and John Ruskin* (Stanford, California: Stanford University Press, 1982) 150, letter 91 and notes

Denmark Hill, S. E.
30th December
1869

Dear Mr. Carlyle,

Partly evil weather, partly my mother's more heavily pressing need of some evening comfort—and the equally pressing need, to me, of the unbroken morning, for what I have to prepare for very real duty at Oxford, have kept me from coming to you.

Might I come at ½ past 8 tomorrow, bringing with me a good, clear-headed, clearsighted—and to you most reverent and faithful—young English Merchant:—the son of my father's nephew[1] —who

1. Apparently William George Richardson (1839–77), the son of Dr. William J. Richardson and the grandson of Ruskin's "Aunt Jessie" Richardson of Perth. In a letter to J. R. Severn on December 30, 1869, (MS: Bembridge) Ruskin says, "Tomorrow George dines with me and we go together to Carlyle's, Bess having long wanted to go. Bess has bought a ship all his own — and calls it the 'Sesame.'" ("Bess" was Ruskin's nickname for George.) In Ruskin, *Diaries*, II, 692, he says, "Jan 1st. Saturday (1870). Last night at Carlyle's with George."

The reference to the *Sesame* is tantalizing. *The Mercantile Navy List, Lloyd's Register,* and other sources say that she was built by John Crown's shipbuilders in Sunderland and launched in February of 1870 for the Sunderland to West Indies run. But the original owner of the ship is listed everywhere as "Hill & Co." of London, with no mention of a Richardson in any connection. Subsequent inquiries have also failed to establish any relationship between Richardson and the schooner. Yet searches in both published and unpublished Ruskin diaries reveal that between 1868 and 1877 Ruskin helped young George in some unidentified business dealings involving thousands of

will I think work with me with all his heart in the sphere of a gradually widening West Indian Commerce—carrying it on, as English commerce should be done. His first ship he has named the "sesame", —she sails her first voyage early in the year. And he has no desire more earnest than that of being permitted to see your face—and hear your voice.

May I bring him?
The Woolwich lecture[2] went well.

Ever your affectionate
J. Ruskin

---

pounds, and the name "Sesame" clearly reveals a connection with Ruskin.

2. "The Future of England," delivered at the Woolwich Arsenal on December 14, 1869, and included in later editions of *The Crown of Wild Olive*.

Another illustration of how footnotes that delineate relationships can be fascinating in themselves, while remaining
only peripheral to the main thesis of an essay, comes from an
undergraduate paper on the relationships, both personal and
political, between Winston Churchill and Franklin Roosevelt.

After substantial introductory material, in which the author
describes, in detail, the background, education, and experience
of the two men before World War II began, and describes their
correspondence and telephone conversations in 1940–1941, the
author narrates the story of their first meeting since the two
had been figures in the naval administration of their respective
countries in World War I. The author discusses the circumstances of the Atlantic Conference, and its result, the "Atlantic
Charter," with considerable elaboration. What might have
proven to be a dry recitation of facts, available from any major
source on the history of the war, is enlivened by a footnote
which shows the familial relationship between the two men.

A student paper

The stage was now set, in Argentia Bay, Newfoundland, for the first face-to-face meeting of the two men as world leaders. The date was August 9, 1941; and the backdrop to the scene was the American heavy cruiser, *Augusta*, which had brought Roosevelt to the rendezvous, and the great British battleship, *Prince of Wales*, newly restored after her confrontation with the *Bismarck*.
The two men really did not know one another's personality well.[1]

1. The two men were, in fact, related to one another through at least three different familial connections. The best known of these is:

Henry Glover, of New Haven, Connecticut (d. 1689)=Helena Russell (d. 1698)

Mercy Glover=Maj. Moses Mansfield   David Ashley=Hannah Glover

Abigail=John Atwater   Nathaniel Lewis=Abigal Ashley

Abigail Atwater=Thomas Hall   Joseph Lyman=Abigail Lewis

Thomas Hall=Lydia Curtis   Joseph Lyman=Mary Sheldon

Mehitable Beach=Ambrose Hall   Anne Jean Robbins=Joseph Lyman

Clarissa Willcox=Ambrose Hall   Warren Delano=Catharine Lyman

Leonard Jerome=Clarissa Hall   James Roosevelt=Sara Delano

Randolph Churchill=Jennie Jerome   FRANKLIN DELANO ROOSEVELT

WINSTON LEONARD SPENCER CHURCHILL

This chart shows them to be, in these lines, seventh cousins, once removed. In other lines, they also were eighth cousins and eighth cousins, twice removed. For additional discussion of these relationships, see Conklin Mann, "Two Famous Descendants of John Cooke and Sarah Warren," *The New York Genealogical and Biographical Record* LXXIII, no. 3 (Fall, 1942): 159–172.

Of course, the types of relationships that you document in footnotes can be more than just those between or among people and the things associated with them. Scientific and mathematical relationships, too, can be the subjects of such notes. Because it is so important, in scientific and technical writing, to keep the central point of your discussion before your reader's eye, no extraneous material must be allowed to interrupt the flow of your text or to disturb the concentration of your reader. So, even the most important secondary materials must be relegated to a footnote. Often, great expositions of scientific principles are marred by an author's tendency to ramble from the subject at hand to lengthy explanations and proofs which are not germane directly to the topic. The great *Principia Mathematica* of Bertrand Russell and Alfred North Whitehead is a masterpiece of dense, but entirely appropriate, rational exposition.[4] As they move from one category of idea to another in their fulsome notation, they restrict all of their asides to small sentences or short paragraphs that are interspersed in the notation—forming a rather different kind of annotation than the one with which most readers are familiar. Nevertheless, Russell and Whitehead provided all subsequent writers in mathematics and the sciences with a lesson in precision and rational order which can be followed, with great profit, by any writer on these subjects.

An excellent example of how a relationship between one element of computation and another can be annotated successfully comes from Petr Beckmann's curious work, *A History of π (PI)*. Near the end of his volume, Beckmann enters into a discussion of the transcendantal nature of π and how Cartesian geometry made it possible to consider π in a new light. If one uses only a ruler and compasses, one can produce curves whose equations are given by polynomials of no more than the second degree. It is from this fact that Beckmann proceeds to elaborate his discussion.

4. Bertrand Russell and Alfred North Whitehead, *Principia Mathematica*, 3 vols. (Cambridge: Cambridge University Press, 1910–1913).

Petr Beckmann, A History of π (PI), 2nd ed. (Boulder,
Colorado: The Golem Press, 1971) 164–165

The points obtained by successive constructions
are therefore always intersections (or tangent
points) of curves of not more than second degree.
We are given a circle whose equation is (we assume unit diameter)

$$4x^2 + 4y^2 = 1$$

and the final result of the construction is to be a
distance equal to π. The coordinates of the end
point of this distance are obtained by a chain of
constructions, each of which amounts to the following: We are given certain points (from the pre-
vious construction) whose coordinates are known
numbers; these coordinates (or their simple functions) become the coefficients of the equation that
is to be solved in the next step, since an intersection involves the solution of two simultaneous
equations.

Starting with

$$4x^2 + 4y^2 = 1$$

and the next step in the construction, characterized by a curve of not more than second degree,
we find the intersection of the two curves by solv-
ing at most a quadratic equation, whose roots are
either rational or irrational numbers involving only
square roots. These roots, or their simple functions, become the coefficients of the equation to
be solved in the next step of the construction. The
next equation is therefore quadratic with coefficients that are either rational or square roots. To
convert this to an equation with rational coeffi-

cients, it is sufficient (and not even necessary) to square the equation twice over, resulting in an equation of not more than 8th degree. If the construction has s steps, the final equation to be solved in order to yield the length π must therefore be an equation with rational coefficients of degree not higher than 8^s, where s is to be finite.[1]

1. This line of reasoning works with sufficient, not necessary conditions. Actually, the final equation will be quadratic, since it can be shown that each new step results in a quadratic equation with coefficients that are either rational or square roots. For details, see Ernest William Hobson, *"Squaring the Circle": A History of the Problem* (Cambridge: Cambridge University Press, 1913); reprinted in *Squaring the Circle, and Other Monographs* ([New York]: Chelsea Publishing Company, 1953) 47–51.

Footnotes for Translations to or from Another Language

WE ALL KNOW the adage that a translation can never fully approach the meaning or the intention of the original. Because that is true, your own translations may well miss a shade of meaning or an image which is perfectly clear in the original, but which is lost in the translation. And translations done by others, no matter how scholarly, are prone to the same errors as your own. How, then, are you going to be sure that your reader understands the material you have quoted with the same fullness as you do, yourself?

Since your reader may know the language from which you got the passage, she may well appreciate the opportunity to read it in its original form, so the best response is to provide her with the text in the original language—and in the script, character, or alphabet of that of language—in a footnote. With a modern wordprocessor, and easy access to so many fonts of so many languages, this is a simple task, although it does require care and meticulous attention to detail.

Perhaps you will prefer to insert the original text in your paper, for the sake of exactness and accuracy. Then what is to become of your reader's search for understanding, if she does not read the language of your passage? The answer, again, is a simple one. You must provide your reader, in such a case, with a translation of the text into the language in which you have written your paper, again, in a footnote.

In either case, a footnote of this type will serve to increase your reader's understanding of the material that you wish to use from a foreign language.

Use footnotes to give either (*a*) the original text of a passage you have translated in the main body of your writing; or (*b*) the translation of a passage that you have used in the main body of your text.

This type of footnote is useful also as a place to put the definition of a word or phrase from a foreign language that you have used in your text in the sense or meaning that it has in that other language. How useful is it for your reader to surmise that YOU seem to know the meaning of the word *Weltanschauung*,[1] because you have used it in your writing, if she has no idea of the meaning of the word in German and no idea, therefore, of your reason for including it in your text.

Our first example of this sort is taken from the leading guidebook to Rome for Catholics in the nineteenth century. Eugène de la Gournerie's book enjoyed extraordinary success in French for decades, because of the meticulous attention to detail that he exhibited in writing about the principal Christian monuments and buildings in Rome.[2] The book's success in French merited a translation into English, from which our excerpt is taken.

Here, the author describes the celebration in Rome on the return of the papal contingent of the Christian fleet which defeated the Turks at the Battle of Lepanto, which was fought on October 7, 1571. The papal admiral, Prince Marcantonio Colonna, was the central focus of a splendid procession.

1. *View of the world* or *world view.*
2. Eugène de la Gournerie, *Rome Chrétien: ou Tableau Historique des Souvenirs et des Monuments Chrétiens de Rome,* 2 vols. (Paris: Librairie de Debecourt, 1843).

Eugène de la Gournerie, *Christian Rome: A Historical View of the Memories and Monuments , 41–1867*, 2 vols., trans. [Alice Edith Middleton,] Lady Macdonald (London: P. Rolandi, 1898), II:221–222

The road selected for this triumphal march passed successively beneath the Arches of Constantine, Titus, and Septimus Severus, all of which had been decorated with inscriptions for the occasion. That on the Arch of Titus was conspicuous; it ran:— "Rejoice, O Jerusalem! Titus Vespasian led thee captive, Pius V endeavors to set thee free."[1] Elsewhere might be read:— "Roman strength is not dead, Roman courage lives forever."[2]

Amid vociferous acclamations the conqueror ascended the Capitol; he was then conducted in state to S. Peter's Basilica, where a Te Deum was sung by the Patriarch of Jerusalem; from thence he proceeded to the Vatican, where he and his prisoners were warmly received by Pius V. The Pontiff uttered words of kindness and consolation, and all the populace, associating themselves with the Pope's action, according to one of the inscriptions "rejoiced in the Lord, on embracing its illustrious and victorious citizen."[3]

1. Lætare, Jerusalem, quam Titus Vespasianus captivam duxit, Pius V liberare contendit.

2. Romanus adhuc viget vigor, Romanaque virtus emicat.

3. Exultans in Domino, clarissimum civem suum victorem, amplectitur Roma.

Our next example, which we chose because it illustrates the significance of providing some reference to important texts in their original languages, is taken from a study of the modern Japanese writer, Ibuse Masuji. Midway through this detailed and critical examination of Masuji's technique, the author turns to a discussion of Masuji's transformation from a writer of short stories to a novelist. He illustrates his discussion with many apposite quotations from Masuji's work, including his novel, *Jon Manjirō hyōryūki*.[3]

In the text itself, A. V. Liman presents his readers with Masuji's text in transliterated Japanese[4] followed immediately by an English translation. The original Japanese text is both cited and presented in the associated note. In this way, every reader has an easy access to the passage, in whatever language brings the greatest degree of understanding.

---

3. *John Manjir,: A Castaway's Chronicle*, based on the dramatic life of Manjiro Nakahama (1827–1898) who was rescued from a shipwreck by an American whaler, was brought to Massachusetts, obtained a full Western education, returned to Japan, and became a leading figure of the Meiji Era. For more about this remarkable man and his career, see Hisakazu Kaneko, *Manjiro, The Man Who Discovered America* (Tokyo: Hokuseido Press, 1954). For a discussion of the shipwreck and rescue, see Emily V. Warinner, "The Ordeal of the Kanrin Maru," in *American Heritage*, vol. XIV, no. 5 (August 1963). And for the story of his son's gift of Nakahama's sword to the town in New England where Nakahama lived and studied, and came to be known as John Manjiro, see *The Presentation of a Samurai Sword: The Gift of Doctor Toichiro Nakahama, of Tokio, Japan, to the Town of Fairhaven, Massachusetts* (Fairhaven: The Millicent Library, 1918). An English translation of Masuji's first successful novel was published in 1947 as *John Manjiro, The Castaway: His Life and Adventures* (Tokyo: Nichei-ei Bunka Kyosha, 1947). A more recent translation can be found in *Castaways: Two Short Novels* (Tokyo: Kodansha International, 1987) where *John Manjiro: A Castaway's Chronicle* is paired with *A Geisha Remembers* [*Oshima no zonnengaki*]; this was, in turn, reprinted in a paperback edition in 1993.

4. Transliteration, as distinct from translation, means, in this case, the rendering of phonetic Japanese in Latin characters.

A[nthony] V. Liman, *A Critical Study of the Literary Style of Ibuse Masuji: As Sensitive As Waters* (Lewiston, [New York]: The Edwin Mellen Press, 1992)

To understand what I have called 'ritualized impersonal narration' we must look at the Japanese text very closely. This is how the original begins: . . .

Chichioya wa Etsusuke to ii, Manjirō kyūsai no toki naku natta.

Manjirō's father, Etsusuke, died when the boy was only eight.

Hahaoya no na o Shio to ii, yamome ni natte kara wa Manjirōra keimai gonin no mono o, onna hitori no te de yōiku shita.

His mother, whom they called Shio, had nothing but her own two hands to raise Manjirō and his four siblings when her husband died.

Mochiron sekihin arau ga gotoki arisama de, kodomo tachi niyomitaki o shikomu yoyū nado arō wake ga nai.[1]

They lived from hand to mouth and one imagines she simply couldn't afford to have her children taught to read and write.

1. Ibuse Masuji, "Jon Manjirō hyōryūki," in *Ibuse Masuji zenshū* (Tokyo: Chikuma shobō, 1974), vol. II, p. 67.

ジョン萬次郎の生まれた故郷は、土佐の間崎多助という漁

村という漁村である。文政十（一八）年の生まれということだ

が、生まれた正確な月日はわからない。父親に悦介と

いう、萬次郎が三歳ごろ亡くなった。母親の名をシヲと

いう、寡婦になってから萬次郎等兄妹主人のものを共

一人の手で養育した。もともと赤貧洗ふが如き有様で、

子供たちに満足な育ちを仕込む余裕などあろうわけがない。

In both of our earlier examples, we used writing in which the original texts that were quoted were placed in the footnotes, and the translations of them were in the main body of the discourse. The next example reverses this arrangement and presents the material from the original language in the discussion itself and places the translation in the footnote. In this case, it is the diction and meter of the original which is the subject of the discussion and the literal meaning in another language is secondary to the discussion—so now the translation appears in the note.

Giulio Rospigliosi (1600–1669) was a poet and librettist of major importance in the first half of the seventeenth century in Rome. Perhaps his most noteworthy act in youth was that he wrote the libretti for the first comic opera in the history of European music, *L'Egisto o Chi soffre speri*. But he was more—an accomplished diplomat, an able administrator, and a leading figure of society. For these reasons, in 1667 he became Pope Clement IX. For this illustration, we chose an excerpt from the most important work about his writing in English, *Operas for the Papal Court with Texts by Giulio Rospigliosi*, by Margaret Kimiko Murata.

Murata begins her dissertation with a brief biography of the "Poet Pope" and continues with an outline history of his libretti. Then, in chapter four, she begins to analyze his literary style, including his poetic meter, his use of rhyme, and his diction and language. Our example is from the opening of the last section.

Margaret Kimiko Murata, "Operas for the Papal Court with Texts by Giulio Rospigliosi" (Ph.D. diss., University of Chicago, 1975) 106

Diction and language

There are several elements that create the diction or tone of a passage. One that affects the musical setting is the length of a complete thought, because this determines the distance between cadences. While far from Milton's rolling lines, this passage from *Erminia* has a certain complicated continuity.

> Satiati homai Fortuna,
> Trionfar pur de' casi miei funesti,
> Che se già mi vedesti
> Là sul famoso Oronte
> Ricco haver d'ostro il manto, e d'or la cuna,
> La scettro in mano,
> E la corona in fronte,
> Qui del Giordano
> In su la riva alpestre
> Di vago scettro in vece
> Porto dardo silvestre,
> E fai, ch'in rozzi ovili
> Io cangi aurati tetti;
> E i popoli soggetti
> Fai, che sieno per me le gregge humili.[1]

1. Now be satisfied, Fortune, likewise triumph over my bad luck, that whether you already saw me there on the famous, rich Orontes with a purple mantle, a cradle of gold, the scepter in hand and a crown on my head, here on the wild banks of the Jordan instead of a lovely scepter, I carry a rustic arrow, and you make me change the golden roofs for rough sheepfolds and make my subject peoples be the humble flocks." From Act II, scene 4.

Cross-References in Footnotes

ONE OF THE most useful kinds of footnotes is a cross-reference to another part of your own paper, where your reader may find more detail about the subject under discussion than she will at the place where you insert the note. The purpose of this type of note, as with all footnotes, is to help your reader to understand your research, analysis, and writing with as little difficulty or inconvenience as possible. This note always should be used sparingly, but it may be necessary on those occasions when you return to a point of discussion at some distance from your original presentation of it, or when you wish to indicate to your reader that some element of your discourse, to which you now make a passing allusion, will be considered in greater detail later in your text. Certainly, you should not need such notes in a short paper of ten, or fifteen, or even twenty pages, but you may well need such notes in a longer presentation, especially one in which you elaborate several points that are closely interwoven with one another.

In these cross-references, there are a few conventional abbreviations which have long been standard and which you should use. More modern writers tend to use the English forms, "see above" and "see below"; while more traditional annotators will use "*vide supra*" and "*vide infra*." If you use the latter, italicize them. For a list of the abbreviations you may need in your cross-references, see appendix B—which is, in itself, as you see, a cross-reference.

Whenever you use a cross-reference note, always be sure to indicate the page number of your own text where the other material can be found—"see above" or "see below" by themselves are not enough.

Because you do need to insert the page number in such notes, they will, of necessity, be the last notes that you will enter in your paper. You may choose to insert the numbers during your original typing, as reminders to fill in the full cross-reference later. Or, you may choose to simply go through the final draft of your paper and insert them just before you print your text. Most wordprocessors show the number of the page on the screen in the lower right corner of your display.

One easy method for constructing your cross-references is to go to the page, or pages, that have the main body of the discussion to which you want to *refer*. Note the number of the page, and then go to that place, or those places, in your text at which you wish to insert references to the main discussion and enter your cross-references. In this way, if you wish to make more than one reference to some part of your discussion, perhaps before the main element of the discourse, perhaps after it, you will place the same numbers in two or more cross-references without any possibility of confusion.

Remember to use cross-references sparingly. If your text is the straightforward, seamless expository writing it should be, you will need to use such a device only rarely, and only when the paper is a longer one with several paths of elaboration.

Expressing Acknowledgments & Thanks

A FOOTNOTE is an ideal place to express your thanks to someone else who may have rescued you from an impasse in your research or who merely volunteered an interesting fact or opinion which you would otherwise have missed. At the same time as it gives you the chance to display courtesy, if offers your reader the name, and, often, the position of a person whom you have found to be well informed on the subject of your paper. In serious research, a student or scholar should speak with the recognized authorities on the subject of that research well before she believes her task is done—always call an expert.[1] By thanking the people with whom you speak, you also inform your reader of your attention to this technique of scholarship and you provide her with the name of someone she can talk to, if she wishes to learn even more about the state of scholarly work in a field today; or, perhaps, if she just wishes to explore the subject for the sake of curiosity. After all, most people, no matter how high their academic or professional position, are eager to speak with anyone who evinces a strong interest in their work.

Of course, the benefits that will accrue to you, if you sincerely acknowledge those who help you, may be incalculable. An old friend of the subject of your biographical paper, herself not a scholar, may be delighted to find her name in print in your writing. Such attention is not flattery, but merely the due of the person who helped you. And you may be rewarded later by further bits of knowledge or further access to unpublished papers and documents, or both.

This particular kind of note also represents the tradition of

1. A good exposition of this technique is in chapter eleven, "Talking to People," in Thomas Mann, *A Guide to Library Research Methods* (New York: Oxford University Press, 1987) 119–132. Most researchers have found that the problem with calling an expert is not getting the person to speak with you but, rather, getting them to stop talking about the subject which commands so much interest in their lives. In former times, of course, such inquiries were by letter, rather than telephone, and we suspect that, in the future, such inquiries, more and more, will be done through electronic mail.

collegiality in academic and professional life. The freshman, as well as the full professor, by her research enters into the community in which ideas and opinions are exchanged freely. By citing the sources of these facts and opinions, just as the writer does in the bibliographic citation, the author acknowledges her debt to this long-standing openness. Of course, this tradition survives in many places outside of academia. In journalism, for example, when a source provides information, she often is mentioned by name in the ensuing article, sometimes with an apposite quotation. The candidness with which information is shared openly is, itself, one of the foundations upon which the whole work of the intellectual life rests. Your footnote, even if it is only one line, plays its part in maintaining this spirit.

In the text below, drawn from the first scholarly article to consider the life of Peter Doyle—Confederate soldier, streetcar operator, and close friend of Walt Whitman—the author expresses his indebtedness to the curator of the Whitman manuscripts in the Library of Congress in Washington. In a conversation, she revealed to him that the Library held the transcript of an interview with Doyle that contained information that was not included in the major published source of information about him. Although this transcript had been published before, the edition was a poor one and, the librarian informed him, there were discrepancies between the manuscript and the published version. Note, again, that the subject of the article is the life of Peter Doyle, not the issue of the accuracy of earlier publications.

At this point in his biography, Murray is describing the circumstances under which Doyle fled from his service in the Confederate Army and made his way to Washington.

Martin G. Murray, "'Pete the Great': A Biography of Peter
Doyle," *Walt Whitman Quarterly Review*, vol. 12, no. 1
(Summer 1994) 9–10

Doyle apparently was ordered to report back to
his company, which was then stationed in Petersburg, Virginia. The records of the Confederate
States Hospital in Petersburg stated that a Peter
Doyle of Dearing's Battalion (the battalion into
which the Fayette Artillery was subsumed) was ad-
mitted on March 19, 1863. The records further
stated that Doyle was released on April 17 to return to duty. At the time of his release from the
hospital, Doyle's company was on duty in Suffolk,
Virginia. According to extant company muster
rolls, Doyle never rejoined his outfit.

What happened next to Doyle? In the Bucke interview, Doyle stated, "Being taken prisoner, hap-
pening in Washington, forced to look out for myself, I stayed in the Capital."[1]

1. For this quote, I have relied on Horace Traubel's handwritten notes of the Doyle interview in the Feinberg Collection
(Container 45), Library of Congress. The published account in
Bucke does not mention Doyle's imprisonment. I am grateful to
Dr. Alice Birney, curator of the Whitman manuscripts at the Library of Congress, for making me aware of the Traubel manuscript, and alerting me to the fact that the manuscript and the
published transcript of the Doyle interview differ in significant
respects.

An author can, if she wishes, use this sort of note to tell her reader about the circumstances under which she made her connection to the person who provided information to her. And she also may describe in detail the nature and scope of that information.

In this way, she clarifies further the precise nature of the help she received and places the results of that assistance into the context of her own research.

One example of this note is to be found in David S. Landes's *Revolution in Time*, from which we excerpted another note, earlier.[2] In the introduction to his work, Landes points out that the idea of a clock has become, for modern science, simply oscillations at certain frequencies. He then expresses his indebtedness for both the idea and the evidence for it to a distinguished senior colleague.

2. David S. Landes, *Revolution in Time: Clocks and the Making of the Modern World* (Cambridge, Massachusetts: The Belknap Press of Harvard University Press, 1983). Note that here we provide a complete citation to Landes's book, even though we did so earlier, because so many pages have passed since our last citation. If we were citing his work often, throughout our book, we would use a shortened form which consists of his name, an abbreviated title, and the relevant page number—Landes, *Revolution*, 6. But, since that is not the case here, we repeat the full citation, so as to spare our reader the necessity of thumbing backwards through our text to find the earlier reference. You should do the same.

David S. Landes, *Revolution in Time: Clocks and the Making of the Modern World* (Cambridge, Massachusetts: The Belknap Press of Harvard University Press, 1983) 6

The desire to avoid dead heats and make possible an ordering of even the closest finishes has led to the introduction of still finer units of measurement. In the 1970s the Olympic Games began using timers calibrated in hundredths of a second that were linked to automatic registers at start and finish. Then, in the winter Olympics at Lake Placid in 1980, the inevitable occurred: the victor in an hours-long cross-country ski race was separated from the second-place finisher by a hundredth of a second. The observer may reasonably ask: Isn't this really a dead heat? Is the margin of error for two pairs of readings taken hours apart significantly smaller than a hundredth of a second? Whatever the answer, the order of finish stood as timed, and one can confidently anticipate the introduction of timers calibrated in thousandths and ten thousandths with a view to avoiding this kind of chronometric and philosophical dilemma.

The demands of sport, of course, are as nothing compared to those of some branches of science. The physicist who seeks to assign times to subatomic events is like the medieval astronomer whose subject matter was running ahead of his instruments. When one enters the world of subatomic particles, one leaves hundredths and thousandths of seconds far behind. This is the world of microseconds (10^{-6}), nanoseconds (10^{-9}), and picoseconds (10^{-12}). These are units invented for purposes of theoretical analysis. Episodes of short duration can in fact be observed and timed by recording and measuring their tracks, as in a cloud chamber, if velocity is known; or can be measured by converting the phenomenon being timed into vibrations (oscillations) and then counting them. Indeed, to the physicist, any stable oscillating phenomenon *is* a clock, and the best of them (the ones with the most stable and highest frequencies) are now the most accurate and precise measuring devices known to science. Today, when the finest measures are desired, such quantities as voltage, mass, and magnetic force are no longer measured in conventional ways but reduced to a frequency determination and then calibrated.[1]

1. I owe this information to Norman F. Ramsey, Higgins Professor of Physics at Harvard University and one of the fathers of atomic timekeeping, whom I had the good fortune to sit next to at a dinner of the Society of Fellows. I want to thank Prof. Ramsey here for the offprints of his publications and for his informative letter of February 17, 1981.

Sometimes, in your research, you will discover an avenue to unpublished, and undocumented, sources that are central to your own work. When you recognize these sources for what they are, when others have overlooked them, you have experienced the gift of serendipity. These new sources may, however, be entirely within the province and custody of an institution which is not one primarily devoted to scholarship and research, like a library or an archive, and, of course, they will not be in the hands of a private person whose aid you would otherwise solicit. In such cases, you must depend on the goodwill and assistance of the staff of the institution for any access you get, and any copying of material you may do. In such a case, it is not only proper, but, in fact, almost mandatory, that you thank the people who made this aspect of your research possible. While you may acknowledge the institution formally on your acknowledgments page, as well as the specific persons who helped you, you should recognize these persons again at the point in your narrative where you make use of the information that they supplied to you.

The example we chose to illustrate this type of footnote is taken from Michael Shelden's biography of George Orwell. Eric Blair, to give Orwell his real name, went to Eton in his youth and, at that famous public school, Shelden discovered a number of papers about Blair's life and experiences there. To use that material, however, the author had to secure permission to see them and then appeal for the right to quote from them. He acknowledges his debt to two members of the staff of Eton who made this possible.

Michael Shelden, *Orwell: The Authorized Biography* (New York: HarperCollins Publishers, 1991) 61–62

At the end of their year in Chamber, his Election moved out of their primitive stalls, and each boy took up residence in a room of his own. For the first time in his school days Blair had some real privacy. And he finally had a good amount of time to spend as he wanted. As a King's Scholar, he was expected to work hard, but the masters tended to let boys develop in their own ways and did not subject them to the kind of bullying and scolding practiced at places like St. Cyprian's. He had had enough of that demanding life and had decided to "slack off and cram no longer." He was true to that resolve. From the first year, his academic work was undistinguished. At the end of the Michaelmas half of 1917 (with supreme indifference to logic, Eton calls its three terms halves), he was at the bottom of his Election's Latin division (class). At the top was Roger Mynors (later Sir Roger Mynors, professor of Latin at Oxford). Mynors had accumulated 520 points from a possible total of 600. Blair's number was 301.[1]

---

1. See Andrew Gow papers (Eton). For permission to examine these papers and for kindly answering my questions about Eton, I am indebted to Dr. Eric Anderson, the headmaster, and Michael Meredith, the school librarian.

Our Grand Finale

EARLIER in our book, we used an excerpt from John Livingston Lowes's masterful study of the pathway taken by Coleridge on his way to his authorship of "The Rime of the Ancient Mariner" and "Kubla Khan," *The Road to Xanadu*. Now, we return to this volume to present a footnote which embodies, almost perfectly, the principles and methods we have tried to illustrate in this little book.

In the first chapter of his work, "Chaos," Lowes recounts how he first came upon a notebook in the British Library that Samuel Taylor Coleridge had written between 1795 and 1798. His experience with these rambling Coleridgian texts ignited the enthusiasm which led to his writing *The Road to Xanadu*. He then presents a few short quotations from the notebook as examples of the material he found in it that illuminated Coleridge's other writing. One of them, a short jotting about alligators, Lowes traced to a book by William Bartram on the latter's travels in the southern United States in the later years of the eighteenth century. In the footnote which accompanies his mention of Bartram, Lowes gives his readers every aspect of his own trail of research into, and thoughts about, a source which influenced Coleridge. He thanks a colleague for guidance to a particular publication that Coleridge read (*The Wonderful Magazine*); he adds an aside on the origins of the Romantic movement ("Alligators were obviously good copy . . ."); he provides corrections for earlier errors by other writers ("A young German scholar shyly corrects . . ."); he provides cross-references to other material in his own book where a greater detail may be found about some of his points ("For the date at which Coleridge first read Bartram . . ."); he points his readers to emendations in Coleridge's own writing, from a time in the poet's life that was far removed from his original reading of Bartram ("In the *Biographia Literaria* . . ."); and he answers many more questions that the interested reader may have about Coleridge's early reading, about the particular use of the alligator image, and about other allusions to Bartram's material in the writings of other poets.

With such a large and ramified body of material, Lowes could have chosen to create an appendix and then to have placed this, and other similar notes, in it. But he offers his readers the opportunity to consider his discoveries directly in association with the text concerning them.

John Livingston Lowes, *The Road to Xanadu: A Study in the Ways of the Imagination* (Boston: Houghton Mifflin Company, 1927) 7–9

Let us begin with the most dramatic moment in the Note Book. Coleridge has been tinkering at some pretty verses, touched here and there with his own elfin magic, about 'Moths in the Moonlight.' Then, without break, he has set down, as if oblivious of the implications of the contrast, one of the most profound and haunting phrases ever penned—

> the prophetic soul
> Of the wide world dreaming on things to come—

and has followed it with a second excerpt from the Sonnets, more poignantly personal than the first:

> Most true it is, that I have look'd on truth
> Askance and strangely.

Next on the page appears a jotting later to find its way, transformed, into the magical opening of 'Christabel':

> Behind the thin
> Grey cloud that cover'd but not hid the sky
> The round full moon look'd small. —

And then, on the heels of a bit of poetized observation of snow curling in the breeze, comes without warning 'the alligators' terrible roar,' and the captivating entry thus proceeds:

> The alligators' terrible roar, like heavy distant thunder, not only shaking the air and waters, but causing the earth to tremble — and when hundreds and thousands are roaring at the same time, you can scarcely be persuaded but that the whole globe is dangerously agitated —

The eggs are layed in layers between of compost of earth, mud, grass, and herbage. — The female watches them — when born, she leads them about the shores, as a hen her chickens — and when she is basking on the warm banks, with her brood around, you may hear the young ones whining and barking, like young Puppies.

20 feet long — lizard-shaped, plated — head vulnerable —tusked — eyes small and sunk —

—Hartley fell down and hurt himself — I caught him up crying and screaming — and ran out of doors with him. — The Moon caught his eye — he ceased crying immediately — and his eyes and the tears in them, how they glittered in the Moonlight! — Some wilderness-plot, green and fountainous and unviolated by Man.

An old Champion who is perhaps absolute sovereign of a little Lake or Lagoon (when 50 less than himself are obliged to content themselves with roaring and swelling in little coves round about) darts forth from the reedy coverts all at once on the surface of the water, in a right line; at first, seemingly as rapid as lightning, but gradually more slowly until he arrives at the center of the lake, when he stops; he now swells himself by drawing in wind and water thro' his mouth, which causes a loud sonorous rattling in the throat for near a minute; but it is immediately forced out again thro' his mouth and nostrils with a loud noise, brandishing his tail in the air, and the vapor ascending from his nostrils like smoke. At other times when swollen to an extent ready to burst, his head and tail lifted up, he twirls round on the surface of the water. He retires — and others, who dare, continue the exhibition — all to gain the attention of the favorite Female —

The distant thunder sounds heavily — the crocodiles answer it like an echo —

Now Coleridge got his alligators from one of the most delightful books which he or anybody ever read, William Bartram's *Travels through North and South Carolina, Georgia, East and West Florida* (the amplitude of the title is prophetic of the book's own leisured pace), *the Cherokee Country, the Extensive Territories of the Muscogulges, or Creek Confederacy, and the Country of the Chactaws*. There is more of the title,[1] but just now the crocodiles and not Bartram hold the stage. Coleridge wanted his alligators badly, but even his genius found them a trifle intractable as boon companions for moths in the moonlight, and in the strange and demon-haunted setting to which he finally transferred them they stubbornly declined to stay.

1. The full title is *Travels through North and South Carolina, Georgia, East and West Florida, the Cherokee Country, the Extensive Territories of the Muscogulges, or Creek Confederacy, and the Country of the Chactaws; containing an Account of the Soil and Natural Productions of those Regions, together with Observations on the Manners of the Indians*. I shall refer throughout to the first edition, Philadelphia, 1791. The crocodile passages are on pp. 127–30, 140. But they also turn up elsewhere. On March 28, 1796, Coleridge drew from the Bristol Library the *Anthologia Hibernica* [: *or Monthly Collections of Science, Belles-Lettres, and History: Illustrated with Beautiful Engravings*, 4 vols. (Dublin: Printed for R. E. Mercier, 1793–1794)], which he kept until April 25 (*Modern Philology*, XXI, 319). And in the first volume of the *Anthologia*, pp. 259–60, is an item of a page and a half entitled 'Crocodiles and their Nests. From *Bartram's Travels*, lately published.' The pages in the Note Book, however (as a comparison show beyond doubt), were not copied from the *Anthologia*. There is also in *The Wonderful Magazine* [:*or New Repository of Wonders*, 5 vols. (London: C. Johnson, 1793–1794)] IV (1793–94), 358, a 'Surprising Account of American Crocodiles,' which is also drawn from Bartram — a piece of information for which I am indebted to Professor A. E. Longueil. Alligators were obviously good copy at the close of the eighteenth cen-

tury. And I should like to seize this opportunity to say at once that those critics who treat the Romantic movement as if it were the brilliant aberration of a group of *literati* would do well to read, mark, and inwardly digest the late eighteenth-century periodicals. For there one gets surprising glimpses of the subterranean streams from which the fountains sprang.

Brandl, in his edition of the Note Book, is silent regarding Coleridge's authority for his alligators; in his life of Coleridge he unluckily is not: 'The notebook of this date contains long paragraphs upon the alligators, boas, and crocodiles of antediluvian times' [Alois Brandl,] (*Samuel Taylor Coleridge, [and the English Romantic School,* ed. Elizabeth Rigby, Lady Eastlake (London: John Murray,)] 1887, p. 202; 'in vorsündflutlichen Lagunen,' [Alois Brandl, *Samuel Taylor Coleridge und die englische Romantik* (Berlin: R. Oppenheim, 1886)] p. 214). Apart from the fact that there are no boas in the Note Book (nor, as distinct from alligators, any crocodiles: 'I have made use of the terms alligator and crocodile indiscriminately for this animal,' says Bartram, p. 90, n., 'alligator being the country name'), one wonders which of the antediluvian patriarchs was supposed to be eye-witness of the scene in the lagoon. A young German scholar shyly corrects in his doctoral dissertation the master's error ([George] Bersch, [*S. T. Coleridges Naturschilderungen in seinen Gedichten* (Marburg: R. Friedrich's Universitäts-Buchdruckerei, 1909)] pp. 75, 101; see below, p. 587, n. 22), and Ernest Hartley Coleridge has already communicated the facts to the Royal Society of Literature (*Transactions,* Second Series, XXVII, 1906, pp. 69–92). As I plunged into the Note Book without waiting (as Carlyle would say) to 'accumulate vehiculatory gear,' I was lucky enough to have the pleasant thrill of discovering for myself the passages in Bartram, before I knew that E. H. Coleridge and Bersch had been ahead of me. The 'green and fountainous wilderness plot' was all that, between them, they had left me. But that turned out to be the richest find of all.

There is another description of alligators in the Carolinas, which Coleridge may or may not have known, in John Lawson's *History of Carolina* [: *containing the exact description and natural history of that country, together with the present state thereof, and journal of a thousand miles, travel'd thro' several nation of Indians, giving a particular account of their customs, manner, &c.*] (London, [Printed for T. Warner,] 1718), pp. 126–28. They are there included, together with Rattle-Snakes, under the heading: 'Insects of Carolina.' Lawson's book is extremely interesting reading, particularly as a companion-piece to Bartram, though its purpose is somewhat less disinterested. For as Thomas Cooper [*Some Information Respecting America* (London: printed for J. Johnson, 1794)](see below, p. 554, n. 57) wrote his book with a view to enticing settlers to the banks of the Susquehanna, so Lawson (see especially pp. 163–67) is urging on prospective colonists the charms of Carolina. And when one reads his chapter 'Of the Vegetables of Carolina' (pp. 89–115) — including 'that noble Vegetable the Vine' — and then goes on to the accounts of game and fish, one wonders that anybody was left in England.

For the date at which Coleridge first read Bartram, see below, p. 513, n. 76. Long after, in 1818, he purchased a copy for himself (*Poems*, I, 460, n. and especially *Transactions of the Royal Society of Literature*, Second Series, 1906, XXVII, 89–90). The edition is that of 1794 [Bartram, *Travels* (London: reprinted for J. Johnson in St. Paul's Church-yard, 1794], and the volume (which I have seen) is in the possession of the Rev. G. H. B. Coleridge. In the *Biographia Literaria* (II, 128–29; cf. 294) he transcribed freely a few lines from the *Travels* (pp. 36–37), with faulty recollection of the name of a tree on pp. 29–30 ('magnolia magni-floria' = magnolia grandiflora). And in T. T. [Samuel Taylor Coleridge, *Specimens of the Table Talk of the late Samuel Taylor Coleridge*, 2 vols. (London: John Murray, 1835)], March 12, 1827 he remarks: 'The latest book of travels I know, written in the spirit of the old travellers, is Bartram's account of his tour in the Floridas.' Wordsworth probably had the volume with him in Germany, for 'Ruth' ('Written in Germany') is saturated with Bartram (see Note 28, below) in such a way as to suggest that the book was a companion of that long and lonely winter. And Bartram was again in Wordsworth's mind when, in 1804, he wrote 'She was a phantom of delight' (compare lines 21–22 of the poem with *Travels*, p. 179, third paragraph).

Conclusion

Now THAT you have come to the end of our little book, we hope that you have a clear and distinct idea of what a good footnote is and how to create it. There is no arcane mystery about them, they are simply a narrative extension, in many forms and styles, of the pathways you took in doing your own research and analysis.

We hope that this book will find a permanent place on your shelf of reference works throughout your days in college, and in all the years beyond as you research and write. We designed this work to be useful not only to the freshman who is receiving her first exposure to the world and the techniques of scholarship but also for serious researchers and writers of all ages who care about documenting their own adventures in scholarship clearly. We also did not limit our ambitions for the work to students in English classes, but rather intended that it should be valuable to students and writers in all of the respectable academic fields, from history to chemistry, from art to physics, and from music to mathematics, the biological sciences, anthropology, and engineering.

In the broadest sense, we hope that this book will serve as another footsoldier in the army which seeks to restore intellectual honesty and openness to expository, non-fictional writing. By revealing completely the whole of your work, you, the author, contribute, directly and personally, to the expansion of knowledge. While we will never know "the whole truth," it is the case that, through these techniques and procedures, we can come just a little bit closer to a true understanding of each problem we, as humanity, tackle.

In the age of rapid access to bibliographical information on the vastest scale, through the Internet and other on-line services; and through the marvelous operation of the great inter-library loan system, each researcher, from the freshman to the professor, from the journalist and the scholar to the hobbyist and the enthusiast, can see, read, and use nearly the whole of the consequence of past writing. The nature of this digital revolution implies, strongly, that every writer on every topic has a real chance to expand upon the whole body of humanity's knowledge of itself and its universe. Materials and opportunities which were once restricted to a favored few in great libraries are now, increasingly, available in the smallest college library and the smallest branch of a public library. With this opportunity, every writer, every student, can contribute significantly to the whole life of the mind. But this contribution can be truly meaningful only if the writer prepares the way for others to take up the task of searching and thinking at the point where the text stops. And this is possible only if the writer meticulously documents her steps so that the new seeker of knowledge stands at an illuminated crossroads with the way ahead clearly indicated.

Appendix A

Adding a Footnote Macro to Your Word Processor

IN THE FOLLOWING paragraphs, we provide specific instructions for writing a macro to place a footnote into your writing automatically. The series of instructions, below, apply to *MS-DOS* and *Windows* software, but, in the case of *Word* and *Word-Perfect 6.1*, they will work equally well on the versions for the *Macintosh*. Some campuses have *WordPectfect 5.1* mounted on *Unix* networks. The instructions we provide here will work perfectly well on the *Unix* version.

Of course, there are many other varieties of word processing software, and it would be impossible to include a suite of instructions for creating a footnote-making macro for each of them. Some, like *Ami Pro 3.1*, come with macro texts which are associated already with specific icons. Please see the manual for your word processor for specific instructions on creating a macro.

A. WORDPERFECT FOR WINDOWS 6.1

To create a macro which will insert a footnote automatically into your paper, use the **left** mouse button to click once on the **Tools** selection from the toolbar. From the drop-down menu, which will now appear, place the cursor over the selection that is labeled **Macro** and click once on it with the **left** mouse button.

A window will open on the right. Place the cursor over the selection that is labeled **Record** and click once on it with the **left** mouse button. A second window now will open. It already will have highlighted the box into which you now can type the name of your new macro. Next, type in *footnote.wcm* and then place the cursor on **Record** and click once on it with the **left** mouse button.

WordPerfect will return you to the main document screen, where the cursor will appear as a circle with a diagonal line in it. At the same time, the text **Macro Record** will appear on the status line at the bottom of your screen, in the left-hand corner.

Now, place the cursor once again on the toolbar, over the selection that is labeled <u>I</u>nsert. Click once on it with the **left** mouse button. From the drop-down menu that appears, place the cursor over the selection that is labeled <u>F</u>ootnote and click on it once with the **left** mouse button. Yet another small window will appear to the right of the drop-down menu. Place the cursor over the selection that is labeled <u>C</u>reate and click on it once with the **left** mouse button.

With the cursor immediately to the right of the superscripted 1 return to the toolbar and again place the cursor over the selection that is labeled <u>T</u>ools and click on it once with the **left** mouse button. The drop-down menu will appear. Now, once again, click once with the **left** mouse button on the bar that is labeled <u>M</u>acro on the menu. Again, a window will open on the right, and you will notice a small check mark to the left of the label <u>R</u>ecord. Move the cursor to that label and click once on it with the **left** mouse button. The check mark will disappear. Use the left button on the mouse to click once in the main document area. Both the small dialog window and the drop-down menu will disappear, and you will have finished creating your macro.

Now that you have created your macro to insert footnotes automatically into your paper, you can make an icon for it and place the icon on your toolbar, so that a single click with the **left** mouse button, when your cursor is on the icon, will place you into the footnote field, ready to insert your text.

First, place the cursor on a blank part of your current toolbar, and then click once with the **right** button of your mouse. Next, in the window which will open, place your cursor over the selection that is labeled <u>P</u>references and click on it once with the **left** mouse button. A second window will open, which has the title **Toolbar Preferences** in the title bar at the top of the window. On the left side of this window, you will see a list of the various toolbars that you can edit. The default toolbar, which is labeled "WordPerfect 6.1." already is highlighted. In the menu, on the right side of this window, place your cursor over the bar that is labeled <u>E</u>dit. Click once on this bar with the **left** mouse button. At this time, yet another window, which has the title **Toolbar Editor** in the title window on top, will open.

Place the cursor inside the smaller box at the lower, right-hand side of this window. The smaller box is labeled **Separator**. Place the cursor inside the box, between the two icons, over the toolbar separator, which has both a down arrow above it and an up arrow below it. The cursor will change from an **arrow** to an **open right hand**. Depress and hold down the **left** mouse button over the dark separator. While holding the **left** mouse button down, drag the separator up to your main toolbar and place it on the right-hand side of your present selection of icons. While you are dragging the separator up to your toolbar, the cursor will change shape, becoming a circle with a diagonal line in it. Release the **left** mouse button, and the separator will drop into place on the right-hand side of the toolbar and the cursor will, once again, become an arrow.

Now, place the cursor inside the window that is entitled **Toolbar Editor**. In the fields that are shown in the upper left of this window, place the **point** of your cursor in the circle to the left of the choice that is labeled **Play a Macro**. Click once with the **left** mouse button and a black dot will fill that circle. At this time, a secondary window will open. It has a bar that is labeled **Add Macro**. Place your cursor on that bar and click once with the **left** mouse button.

Another window will appear, with the title **Select Macro** in the bar on top. Place your cursor on the down arrow to the lower right of the alphabetical list of macros at the left of the window. Depress the **left** mouse button and hold it down, until the macro you created, *footnote.wcm*, appears in the window. Place the cursor on the words *footnote.wcm* and click once with the **left** mouse button. Now, move the cursor to the upper right-hand corner of this window, over the bar that is labeled **Select**, and then click once with your **left** mouse button.

Another window will open which asks you whether or not you wish to save the macro with its full path. Place the cursor over the bar which is labeled **Yes** and click once with the **left** mouse button.

At this point, you will be returned to the window entitled **Toolbar Editor**. Move your cursor to the bar in the upper right-hand corner of the window which is labeled **OK**, and click once with the **left** mouse button.

WordPerfect now will return you to the window that is entitled **Toolbar Preferences**. Place the cursor over the bar in the window that is labeled <u>C</u>lose and click once with the **left** mouse button.

Once again, you will be in the main document window, where, at a superficial glance, everything appears to be the same as it was when you started this process. However, a closer look will show you a new icon at the right-hand side of the toolbar. Place your cursor on that icon and notice a little yellow window open with the word **Footnote**. Click here with your **left** mouse button whenever you wish to insert a footnote into your paper.

B. MICROSOFT WORD FOR WINDOWS 6.0

To create a macro which will insert a footnote automatically into your paper, use the left mouse button to click once on the word **Tools** on the menu line above your document. A dropdown menu now will appear. Move your mouse's cursor down the list of terms on the menu until you find the word <u>Cus</u>tomize. Click once on that word. A window will open with the word **Customize** in the active window display at the top. From the dialog box that labelled **Categories** on the left-hand side of this window, click once with your left mouse button on the word **Insert**. A group of sixteen buttons will appear in the dialog box that is labelled Buttons near the center of the **Customize** window. Place your cursor on the second button from the left in the top row. It has a design that looks like this: **AB**[1]. Place the mouse's cursor on that icon and press **and hold** the left mouse button. Now drag the icon rightward and upward to the toolbar and place this button on the same row that is occupied by the active buttons that already are there. Release the left mouse button. Return to the window that is labelled **Customize** and place the cursor on the word **Close** in the bar on the upper right-hand corner of the window. Click once with your left mouse button and the windows will vanish. Your icon is now in place and ready for you to use each time you wish to add a footnote.

Microsoft Word for Windows 6.0 has one procedure that is somewhat different from that used by other wordprocessing programs. When you have finished typing your footnote, you must click once on the bar which contains the word **Close**, just above the footnote window.

C. WORDPERFECT 5.1 FOR DOS

Before you begin to create your macro for footnotes, you need to be aware of the following conventions in these directions for making a footnnote macro in Wordperfect 5.1 for DOS.

In these directions, when we say **Ctrl-F10**, we mean that you should **depress and hold down** the key that is labeled **Ctrl**, which often is to be found at the lower left-hand corner of your keyboard, and **then** press the F10 key, which is to be found either on the top row of keys on the keyboard or, on some older styles of keyboards, at the left-hand side.

Similarly, when we say **Alt-F**, we mean that you should **depress and hold down** the key that is labeled **Alt**, which can be found on the bottom row of the keys on your keyboard, and **then** press the key for the letter **F**.

Often, you can find two **Ctrl** and two **Alt** keys on your keyboard, one each to the right and left of your spacebar.

First, at the DOS prompt [C:\DIRECTORY NAME], start WordPerfect 5.1 by typing **wp** and pressing the **Enter** key. A blank work screen now will appear, probably with a status line, on which you will see the number of the current document and your place in that document, at the lower right corner of the screen. You now are ready to begin to record your macro.

First, press **Ctrl-F10**. The words "*Define macro:*" will appear in the lower left corner of the screen. Now, depress the **Alt** key and then a letter key to establish which combination of keystrokes you will use each time you wish to insert a footnote in your paper. We suggest that you choose **Alt-F** —"*f*" for footnote—because it is an easy one to remember; but, if the **Alt-F** combination already is being used, select another that you will remember easily. This **Alt-key** combination will become your "hot key" for your footnote macro.

Now, the word "*Description:*" will appear on the status line at the lower left corner of your screen. Type in the words: "*Insert Footnote*" and press the **Enter** key. The words "*Macro Def*" will appear, flashing, on the status line at the lower left corner of your screen.

You now are ready to record the keystrokes of your macro. Press the keystrokes described below precisely in the order in which they appear:

⇨ **Ctrl-F7**
⇨ 1 (the numeral "1" at the upper left corner of your keyboard)
⇨ 1 (the numeral "1" at the upper left corner of your keyboard)

At this point, the words "*Footnote: Press Exit when done*" will appear to the left of the flashing text: "*Macro Def.*" You now are ready to complete your macro.

Press **Ctrl-F10** again, to turn off the macro recording feature. The job is done.

Note that you now are in the footnote field, where you will type your footnotes when you write your paper. To leave the footnote field, you must press **F7**, which is the **Exit** key in WordPerfect 5.1 for DOS. Press **F7** now. You will press the **F7** key at the end of every footnote you write. This action will return you to the text of your paper, where you will see the footnote number highlighted in a small oblong box at the point in your paper at which the superscripted footnote number will appear when you print your paper. The text of the footnote itself, of course, will appear at the bottom of the page, when you print it.

Now that you have created your footnote macro, you can close Wordperfect altogether. To do this, press the following keys in the precise order that is shown here:

⇨ **F7**
⇨ **n**
⇨ **y**

Your footnote macro is waiting for you to write your text.

Appendix B
List of Abbreviations Frequently Found in Footnotes

THE FOLLOWING LIST includes most, but not all, of the abbreviations which are found commonly in footnotes. As you will see from the fact that so many of them are Latin abbreviations, the use of these terms is both hallowed and traditional. Do familiarize yourself with them and use them appropriately. Most well-informed readers are used to seeing them and expect certain kinds of information to be conveyed to them through their use. Those which are Latin in themselves—*cf., i. e., e. g., etc., ca., et al., ibid., q. v., and s. v.*, and some others—should be italicized in your text.

In addition to these abbreviations, there are some others which are standard. Among them are abbreviations for the books and versions of the Bible;[1] the plays of Shakespeare, the works of Geoffrey Chaucer, and some other literary works.[2] In addition, the writer and reader of footnotes should have a good familiarity with Roman numerals and the Greek alphabet.

The most complete source of information about abbreviations and acronyms of all kinds, including the recognized forms for abbreviating the titles of scholarly journals, is the *Acronyms, Initialisms, & Abbreviations Dictionary* published by Gale Research in Detroit, Michigan.[3] It is an annual, so you should search for the latest edition.

abbr.: abbreviated, -ion
ab init.: *ab initio*, from the beginning
abr.: abridged; abridgment
add.: addendum

---

1. *The Chicago Manual of Style*, 14th ed., (Chicago: The University of Chicago Press, 1993) §§14.34 and 14.35, pp. 474–477; or Joseph Gibaldi, *MLA Handbook for Writers of Research Papers*, 4th ed., (New York: The Modern Language Association of America, 1995) §6.7.1, pp. 222–225.

2. Gibaldi, *MLA Handbook*, §§6.7.2, 6.7.3, 6.7.4, pp. 225–227.

3. *Acronyms, Initialisms, & Abbreviations Dictionary*, 20th ed. (Detroit, Michigan: Gale Research, Inc., 1995).

ad inf.: *ad infinitum*, to infinity
ad init.: *ad initium*, at the beginning
ad int.: *ad interim*, in the meantime
ad lib.: *ad libitum*, at will
ad loc.: *ad locum*, at the place
æt.: *aetatis*, aged
anon.: anonymous
app.: appendix
art.: article
b.: born; brother
bibl.: *bibliotheca*, library
bibliog.: bibliography, -er, -ical
biog.: biography, -er, -ical
bk.: block; book
c.: chapter (in law citations); *circa*
ca.: *circa*, about, approximately
Cantab.: *Cantabrigiensis*, of Cambridge
cf.: *confer*, compare
chap.: chapter
Cia: *Compañia*, Company (no period)
Cie: *Compagnie*, Company (no period)
col.: column
colloq.: colloquial, -ly, -ism
comp.: compiler (*pl.* comps.); compiled by
cont.: continued
copr.: cop., or ©, copyright
cp.: compare
d.: died; daughter
dept.: department
d.h.: *das heisst*, namely
d.i.: *das ist*, that is
dial.: dialect
dict.: dictionary
dim.: diminutive
div.: division; divorced
do.: ditto (the same)
dram. pers.: *dramatis personæ*
Dr. u. Vrl.: *Druck und Verlag*, printer and publisher
D.V.: *Deo volente*, God willing
ea.: each
ed. editor (*pl.* eds.); edition; edited by

e.g.: *exempli gratia*, for example
encyc.: encyclopedia
engr.: engineer; engraved, engraving
esp.: especially
et al.: *et alii*, and others
etc.: &c., *et cetera*, and so forth
et seq.: *et sequentes*, and the following
ex.: example (*pl.* exx. *or* exs.)
f.: and following (*pl.* ff.)
fasc.: fascicle
fig.: figure
fl.: *floruit*, flourished
fol.: folio
fr.: from
f.r.: *folio recto*, on the front of the page
fut.: future
f.v.: *folio verso*, on the back of the page
ibid.: *ibidem*, in the same place[4]
id.: *idem*, the same
i.e.: *id est*, that is
incl.: inclusive; including; includes
inf.: *infra*, below
inst.: instant, this month; institute, institution
introd. or intro,: introduction
irreg.: irregular
l.: left; line (*pl.* ll.)
lang.: language
lit.: literally
loc.: locative
loc. cit.: *loco citato*, in the place cited
loq.: *loquitur*, he or she speaks

4.   A wonderful bird is the *ibid*.
         In appearance it's pale and insibid.
         It stands as a sage
         At the foot of the page
         To tell where the passage was cribbed.

See Richard D. Altick, *The Art of Literary Research*, 3d. ed., rev John J. Fenstermaker (New York: W. W. Norton & Company, 1981) 226; quoting *A News Letter of the Institute of Early American History & Culture* (June 1958), no. 13.

m.: married; male; measure (pl. mm.)
marg.: margin, -al
med.: median; medical; medieval; medium
memo: memorandum
mimeo.: mimeograph
misc.: miscellaneous
m.m.: *mutatis mutandis*, necessary changes being made
MS (*pl.* MSS): *manuscriptum* (-*a*), manuscript(s)
mus.: museum; music, -al
n.: *natus*, bom; note, footnote (*pl.* nn.); noun
N.B.: *nota bene*, take careful note
n.d.: no date
no.: number (*pl.* nos.)
non obs.: *non obstante*, notwithstanding
non seq.: *non sequitur*, it does not follow
n.p.: no place; no publisher; no page
N.S.: New Style (dates)
n.s.: new series
ob.: *obiit*, died
obs.: obsolete
op. cit.: *opere citato*, in the work cited
O.S.: Old Style (dates)
o.s.: old series
Oxon.: *Oxoniensis*, of Oxford
p.: page (*pl.* pp.); past
par.: paragraph
pass.: *passim*, throughout; here and there; passive
perf.: perfect; perforated
perh.: perhaps
pers.: person, personal
pinx.: *pinxit*, painted by
pl.: plate; plural
PPS: *post postscriptum*, a later postscript
pres.: present
pro tem.: *pro tempore*, for the time being
prox.: *proximo*, next month
PS: *postscriptum*, postscript
pt.: part
pub.: publication, publisher, published by
quart.: quarterly
q.v.: *quod vide*, which see

R.: *rex*, king; *regina*, queen; right (in stage directions)
r.: right; reigned; recto
repr.: reprint, reprinted
rev.: review; revised, revision
s.a.: *sine anno*, without year; *sub anno*, under the year
sc.: scene; *scilicet*, namely; *sculpsit*, carved by
sec.: section; *secundum*, according to
ser.: series
s.l.: *sine loco*, without place
s.n.: *sine nomine*, without name
st.: stanza
subj.: subject; subjective; subjunctive
sup.: *supra*, above
supp. *or* suppl., supplement
s.v.: *sub verbo*, *sub voce*, under the word (*pl.* s.vv.)
ult.: *ultimatus*, ultimate, last; *ultimo*, last month
univ.: university
usw.: *und so weiter*, and so forth
ut sup.: *ut supra*, as above
v.: verse (*pl.* vv.); verso; versus; *vide*, see
viz.: *videlicet*, namely
vol.: volume
vs. *or* v.: versus
yr.: year; your